THE HAMMER
AND
THE ANVIL

THE HAMMER

AND

THE ANVIL

FREDERICK DOUGLASS, ABRAHAM LINCOLN, AND THE END OF SLAVERY IN AMERICA

DWIGHT JON ZIMMERMAN • ILLUSTRATED BY WAYNE VANSANT

FOREWORD BY

JAMES M. McPHERSON

EDITORIAL CONSULTANT CRAIG SYMONDS

A Novel Graphic from Hill and Wang

A division of Farrar, Straus and Giroux

New York

Hill and Wang
A division of Farrar, Straus and Giroux
18 West 18th Street, New York 10011

This is a Z File, Inc. Book
Text copyright © 2012 by Dwight Jon Zimmerman
Artwork copyright © 2012 by Wayne Vansant
Foreword copyright © 2012 by James M. McPherson
All rights reserved
Distributed in Canada by D&M Publishers, Inc.
Printed in the United States of America
First edition, 2012

Library of Congress Cataloging-in-Publication Data
Zimmerman, Dwight Jon.
    The hammer and the anvil : Frederick Douglass, Abraham Lincoln, and the end of slavery in
America / Dwight Jon Zimmerman and Wayne Vansant. — 1st ed.
        p.   cm.
    "A novel graphic from Hill and Wang."
    ISBN 978-0-8090-5358-2 (alk. paper)
    1. Douglass, Frederick, 1818-1895—Comic books, strips, etc. 2. Lincoln, Abraham, 1809-
1865—Comic books, strips, etc. 3. Antislavery movements—United States—History—19th
century—Comic books, strips, etc. 4. African American abolitionists—Biography—Comic
books, strips, etc. 5. Presidents—United States—Biography—Comic books, strips, etc. 6.
Graphic novels. I. Vansant, Wayne. II. Title.

E449.D75Z56 2012
973.7092'2—dc23
[B]
                                                                                    2011032361

Editor: Howard Zimmerman
Design: Kevin Cannon

www.fsgbooks.com

1 3 5 7 9 10 8 6 4 2

To James A. Salicrup, my friend and mentor.

—DWIGHT JON ZIMMERMAN

In memory of Mary Wilson McLarty, my great-, great-, great-, great-grandmother, born in Ireland in 1776, died in Douglas County, Georgia, in 1866, buried in Dark Corner, where she is surrounded by the markers of eleven grandsons, all killed in the American Civil War.

—WAYNE VANSANT

CONTENTS

FOREWORD

Abraham Lincoln and Frederick Douglass were two of the most famous Americans of the nineteenth century. Together they provided much of the leadership that brought an end to slavery in the United States. Yet they did not meet each other for the first time until August 1863, when Lincoln was fifty-four years old and Douglass was forty-five. On that occasion, Douglass urged equal treatment for black soldiers fighting for the Union in the Civil War. Lincoln promised to do what he could to assure such treatment, and mostly made good on that promise.

This meeting reflected the positions and actions of the two men. Douglass was an abolitionist, a radical reformer, and an eloquent speaker who made a career of demanding freedom, justice, and equal rights for black people. As president of the United States and commander in chief of the armed forces of the Union, Lincoln could exert his power to accomplish these goals, but had to balance the interests and viewpoints of many different groups and could not always fulfill every demand of abolitionists like Douglass.

Both men were born in obscure and humble circumstances. Lincoln's parents were farmers on the Kentucky and Indiana frontier. His mother died when he was nine years old. His relations with his father were often difficult. Frederick Bailey (he later changed his name to Douglass) was born a slave in Maryland. His mother died when he was seven years old, and he never knew his father. Both boys were ambitious to get ahead. Lincoln learned to read and write mostly on his own, and so did Douglass. Lincoln eventually became a lawyer, and moved up in the world of politics until he was elected president in 1860. Douglass escaped from slavery. He became a powerful speaker and newspaper editor, speaking and writing eloquent words for freedom.

As an abolitionist, Douglass called for immediate and universal freedom for the four million slaves. Lincoln hated slavery as much as Douglass did, but he considered the abolitionist program extreme and unrealistic. He opposed the expansion of slavery into the territories and new states, in the expectation that such restrictions would be the first step toward the ultimate end of slavery.

Many white people in the slave states considered Lincoln's anti-slavery position just as radical as Douglass's abolitionism. When Lincoln was elected president in 1860, seven slave states seceded and formed the Confederate States of America. Four more went out after the Civil War began when the Confederates fired on Fort Sumter. Thereafter, Lincoln's and Douglass's positions converged, until, with the Emancipation Proclamation of January 1, 1863, and the Thirteenth Amendment to the Constitution in 1865, Lincoln and Douglass stood together.

In words and drawings, this book tells the dramatic stories of these two famous men, and how they eventually brought freedom to four million slaves and ended the institution of slavery that had made a mockery of American claims to be a land of liberty. Thanks to them more than to anyone else, America **DID** become a land of liberty in 1865.

James M. McPherson

THE HAMMER

AND

THE ANVIL

Chapter One:
The Early Years

ABRAHAM LINCOLN WAS BORN IN THE FIRST DECADE OF THE 19th CENTURY.

FREDERICK DOUGLASS WAS BORN IN ITS SECOND DECADE.

NEGROES FOR SALE

LIKE THE NEW CENTURY, THE YOUNG REPUBLIC CALLING ITSELF THE **UNITED STATES OF AMERICA** SEEMED FULL OF PROMISE AND BOUNDLESS **OPPORTUNITY**. IN ONLY FORTY YEARS, THE NEW NATION HAD ROUGHLY TRIPLED IN SIZE.

FOR AMERICAN **CITIZENS**, IT SEEMED THE ONLY BOUNDARY KEEPING THEM FROM ACHIEVING THEIR **DREAMS** WAS THE LIMIT OF THEIR OWN **IMAGINATION**. SUCH WAS THE GLOWING REALITY INTO WHICH ABRAHAM LINCOLN WAS BORN TO A POOR KENTUCKY HOMESTEADER ON FEBRUARY 12, 1809.

THE REALITY WAS QUITE **DIFFERENT** FOR THOSE IN AMERICA WHO WERE NOT CITIZENS...THOSE WHO WERE CONSIDERED TO BE **MORE PROPERTY THAN PEOPLE**. AS FREDERICK DOUGLASS (WHO GREW UP WITH THE NAME **FREDERICK BAILEY**) WOULD DISCOVER, THE TRAITS OF INTELLIGENCE, IMAGINATION, AND AMBITION -- SO ADMIRED AND DESIRED IN WHITES -- WERE TO BE **BEATEN OUT** OF NEGRO SLAVES.

AUTUMN 1818. PERRY COUNTY, INDIANA.

THE PIGEON CREEK HOMESTEAD OF **THOMAS LINCOLN**.

OH, MAMA! PLEASE DON'T DIE!

THOMAS HAD BROUGHT HIS WIFE, NANCY, DAUGHTER, SARAH, AND SON, ABRAHAM, HERE FROM KENTUCKY IN 1816. IT WAS A PLACE YOUNG ABE LINCOLN WOULD COME TO **HATE**.

IN LATE SEPTEMBER, **NANCY LINCOLN** CAME DOWN WITH **BRUCELLOSIS**, KNOWN LOCALLY AS THE **MILK SICKNESS**. IT WAS CONTRACTED WHEN FREE-ROAMING COWS ATE THE POISONOUS **WHITE SNAKEROOT PLANT**. THE **POISON** WAS PASSED ALONG TO PEOPLE THROUGH THE COWS' MILK. IT WAS ALMOST ALWAYS FATAL.

MAMA...

IT HAD ALREADY CLAIMED THE **LIVES** OF A NUMBER OF PEOPLE IN THE AREA, INCLUDING NANCY'S AUNT AND UNCLE, **ELIZABETH AND THOMAS SPARROW**. NOW NANCY WAS **DYING**.

I AM GOING AWAY FROM YOU, ABRAHAM, AND I SHALL NOT RETURN.

THE WOMAN WHO HAD TAUGHT ABRAHAM LINCOLN TO READ AND LOVE BOOKS, WHOM HE LATER RECALLED AS HIS "ANGEL MOTHER," DIED ON **OCTOBER 5, 1818**.

HE WAS NINE YEARS OLD.

THE NEXT DAY, THOMAS LINCOLN PERFORMED HIS **FINAL DUTY** FOR HIS WIFE. TOGETHER WITH SOME HELP FROM ABE, HE BUILT A **WOODEN COFFIN** FOR NANCY.

HOLD THE BOARDS STEADY, ABRAHAM.

YES, FATHER.

NANCY WAS BURIED BESIDE HER AUNT AND UNCLE IN A **PRIVATE CEMETERY** ON A SMALL HILL NEAR THE HOMESTEAD. THE LINCOLNS WERE **SEPARATIST BAPTISTS**, A FAITH THAT BELIEVED LIFE WAS A PREPLANNED PATH FILLED WITH STRUGGLE. THEIR HARDSCRABBLE LIFE, AND NANCY'S TRAGIC DEATH, SEEMED TO CONFIRM THAT BELIEF.

"MAN...LIKE AN EMPTY SHADOW, GLIDES AWAY, AND ALL HIS LIFE IS BUT A WINTER'S DAY."

IN DECEMBER 1819, THOMAS LINCOLN **MARRIED** THE WIDOW **SARAH BUSH JOHNSTON,** WHO HAD THREE GROWN CHILDREN. AMONG THIS KIND AND PRACTICAL WOMAN'S **POSSESSIONS** WAS ONE THING THAT TRANSPORTED ABE TO **RAPTURE**--

AND I BROUGHT ALL MY BOOKS.

-- A SMALL BUT EXCELLENT **LIBRARY.**

I THINK YOU WILL LIKE THIS BOOK, ABRAHAM. IT IS CALLED PILGRIM'S PROGRESS.

IT'S ABOUT A YOUNG MAN NAMED CHRISTIAN AND HOW HE BETTERS HIMSELF.

ABE FOUND IT TO BE A RIVETING BOOK. YOUNG CHRISTIAN'S STRUGGLES IN LIFE WERE SOMETHING HE EASILY IDENTIFIED WITH.

SHE'S **RIGHT!** HE'S LIKE ME!

UNTIL HE REACHED HIS **MAJORITY** AT AGE 21, ABE LINCOLN WAS SUBJECT TO HIS FATHER'S ORDERS.

WORK HARD, NOW, ABRAHAM!

THOMAS LINCOLN FREQUENTLY **HIRED OUT** HIS SON TO NEIGHBORING FARMERS, FOR WHICH THOMAS, NOT ABRAHAM, RECEIVED PAYMENT.

GOT TO FINISH THIS CHAPTER...

...BEFORE I REACH THE FIELD.

NOW, **THAT'S** INTERESTING!

THOMAS WAS **EXPLOITING** HIS SON IN THE SAME WAY SLAVE OWNERS DID THEIR SLAVES. YOUNG ABRAHAM HATED THE SITUATION, BUT AT THAT AGE THERE WAS **NOTHING** HE COULD DO TO CHANGE IT.

AS AN ADULT, LINCOLN WOULD ADMIT THIS **EXPERIENCE** HAD LAID THE FOUNDATION FOR HIS **HATRED** OF SLAVERY.

FATHER WORKS ME LIKE A SLAVE... BUT AT LEAST I'M FREE TO READ!

HIS BEING HIRED OUT AS A CHILD RESULTED IN A LACK OF **FORMAL EDUCATION**, SINCE IT WAS CONTINUALLY INTERRUPTED AND ULTIMATELY TOTALED LESS THAN A **YEAR**.

BUT AS HIS HALF SISTER MATILDA LATER RECALLED, "ABE WAS NOT ENERGETIC EXCEPT IN ONE THING, HE WAS ACTIVE AND PERSISTENT IN **LEARNING** -- READ EVERYTHING HE COULD."

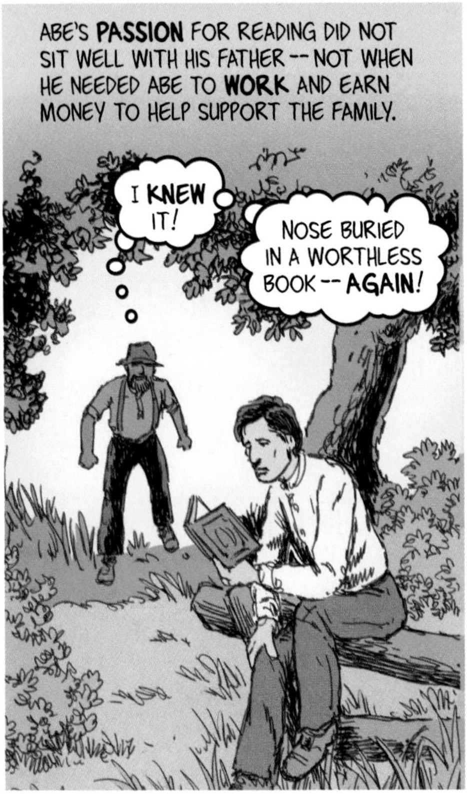
ABE'S **PASSION** FOR READING DID NOT SIT WELL WITH HIS FATHER -- NOT WHEN HE NEEDED ABE TO **WORK** AND EARN MONEY TO HELP SUPPORT THE FAMILY.
I **KNEW** IT!
NOSE BURIED IN A WORTHLESS BOOK -- **AGAIN**!

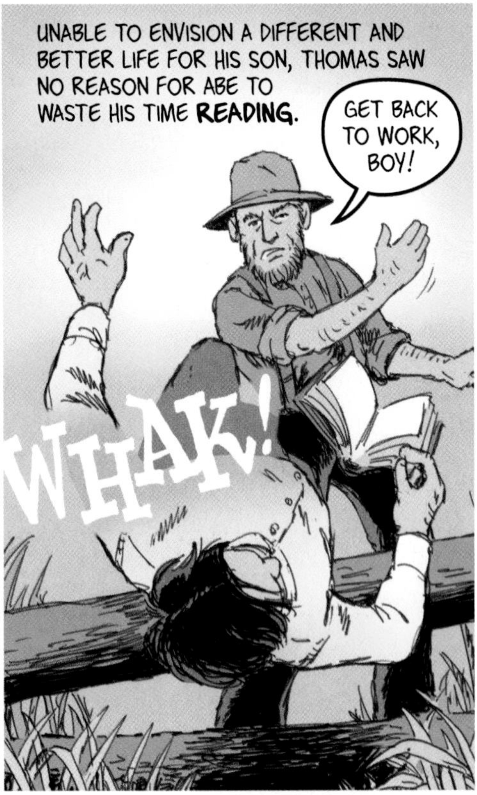
UNABLE TO ENVISION A DIFFERENT AND BETTER LIFE FOR HIS SON, THOMAS SAW NO REASON FOR ABE TO WASTE HIS TIME **READING**.
GET BACK TO WORK, BOY!
WHAK!

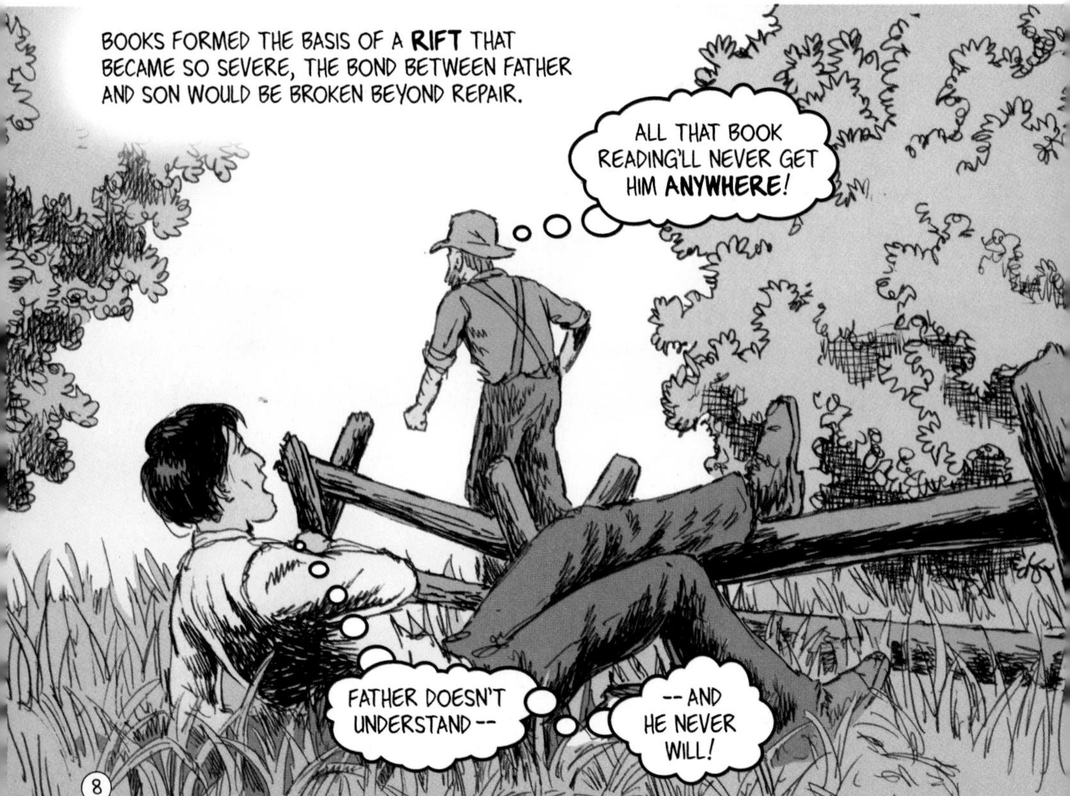
BOOKS FORMED THE BASIS OF A **RIFT** THAT BECAME SO SEVERE, THE BOND BETWEEN FATHER AND SON WOULD BE BROKEN BEYOND REPAIR.
ALL THAT BOOK READING'LL NEVER GET HIM **ANYWHERE**!
FATHER DOESN'T UNDERSTAND --
-- AND HE NEVER WILL!

TALBOT COUNTY, MARYLAND. AUGUST 1824.

BETSEY BAILEY WAS A FISHING-AND-FARMING **LEGEND** AMONG THE LOCALS. HER HANDWOVEN NETS WERE IN HIGH DEMAND, AS WERE HER ADVICE AND FIELD HELP IN PLANTING AND HARVESTING.

YOU STAY CLOSE, FREDERICK!

YES, GRANDMAMMY!

A **SLAVE WOMAN** LIVING WITH THE FREEMAN ISAAC BAILEY, BETSEY WAS RESPONSIBILE FOR THE CARE OF HER GRANDCHILDREN. HER FIVE DAUGHTERS, JENNY, ESTHER, MILLY, PRISCILLA, AND HARRIET, LABORED FOR THEIR ABSENTEE MASTER, **CAPTAIN AARON ANTHONY.** CAPTAIN ANTHONY LIVED AT THE NEARBY WYE HOUSE PLANTATION, WHERE HE WORKED AS OVERSEER FOR ITS OWNER, COLONEL EDWARD LLOYD.

WHEN HER **GRANDCHILDREN** WERE ABOUT THE AGE OF SIX, BETSEY BAILEY WOULD TAKE THEM BY THE HAND TO THE **GREAT HOUSE**, AS A MASTER'S HOME WAS CALLED. IN THIS CASE, IT WAS CAPTAIN ANTHONY'S HOME AT THE WYE HOUSE PLANTATION.

WHAT'S **THAT**, GRANDMAMMY?

IT'S THE **GREAT HOUSE!**

IT'S THE BIGGEST THING I EVER SAW!

SHE DID NOT TELL HER YOUNGEST GRANDCHILD, FREDERICK BAILEY, WHY THEY WERE TRAVELING TO THE GREAT HOUSE. HE WOULD DISCOVER THE REASON SOON ENOUGH.

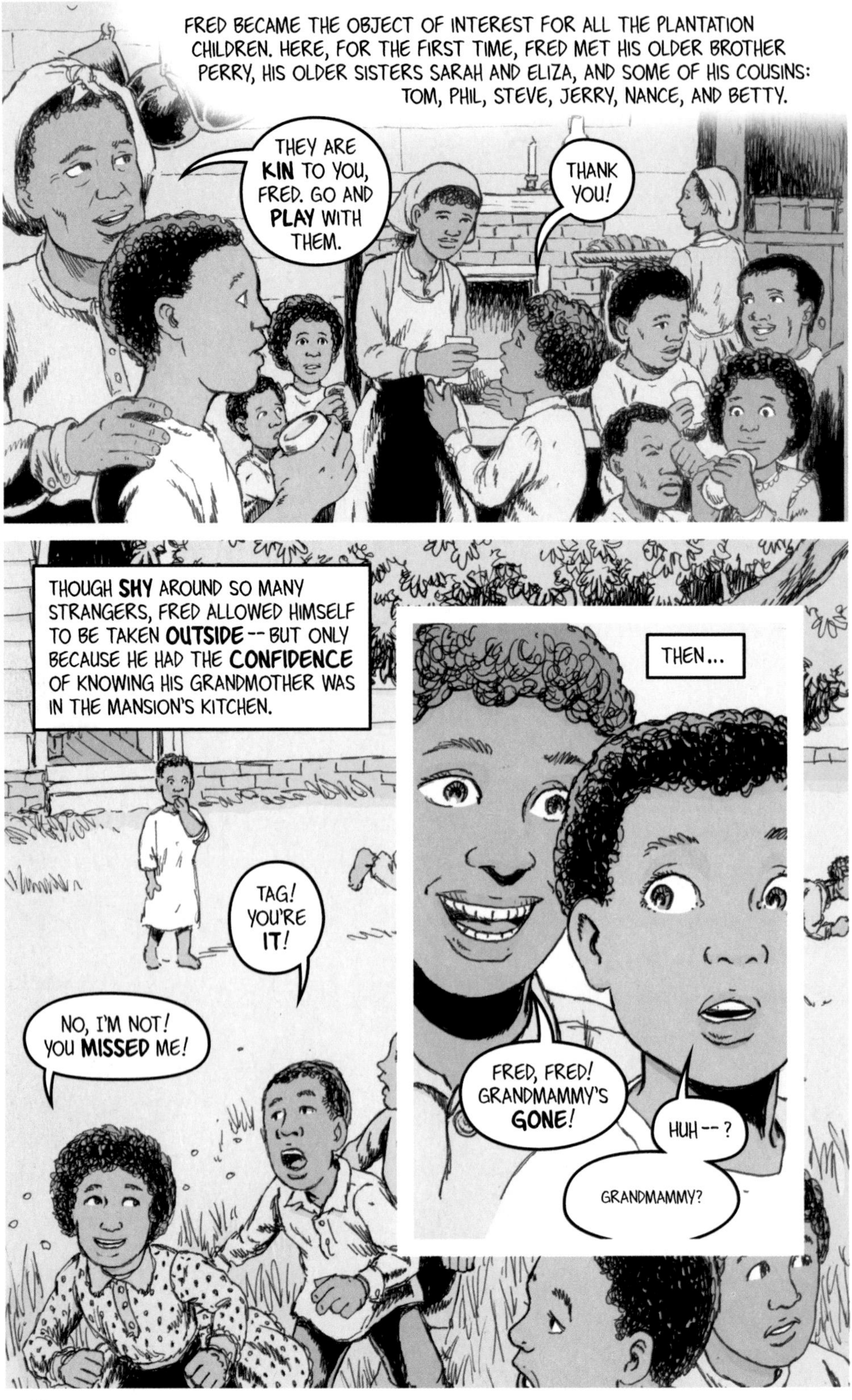
FRED BECAME THE OBJECT OF INTEREST FOR ALL THE PLANTATION CHILDREN. HERE, FOR THE FIRST TIME, FRED MET HIS OLDER BROTHER PERRY, HIS OLDER SISTERS SARAH AND ELIZA, AND SOME OF HIS COUSINS: TOM, PHIL, STEVE, JERRY, NANCE, AND BETTY.
THEY ARE **KIN** TO YOU, FRED. GO AND **PLAY** WITH THEM.
THANK YOU!
THOUGH **SHY** AROUND SO MANY STRANGERS, FRED ALLOWED HIMSELF TO BE TAKEN **OUTSIDE**--BUT ONLY BECAUSE HE HAD THE **CONFIDENCE** OF KNOWING HIS GRANDMOTHER WAS IN THE MANSION'S KITCHEN.
TAG! YOU'RE **IT**!
NO, I'M NOT! YOU **MISSED** ME!
THEN...
FRED, FRED! GRANDMAMMY'S **GONE**!
HUH--?
GRANDMAMMY?

YEARS LATER, IN HIS **AUTOBIOGRAPHY** *THE LIFE AND TIMES OF FREDERICK DOUGLASS,* HE WROTE: "THIS WAS MY FIRST **INTRODUCTION** TO THE REALITIES OF THE **SLAVE SYSTEM.**"

"MY ONLY RECOLLECTIONS OF MY OWN **MOTHER** ARE OF A FEW **HASTY VISITS** MADE IN THE NIGHT ON FOOT, AFTER THE DAILY TASKS WERE OVER, AND WHEN SHE WAS UNDER THE NECESSITY OF RETURNING IN TIME TO RESPOND TO THE DRIVER'S CALL TO THE **FIELD** IN THE EARLY MORNING…"

"SHE **DIED** WHEN I WAS ABOUT **SEVEN YEARS OLD**…I WAS **NOT ALLOWED** TO BE PRESENT DURING HER ILLNESS, AT HER DEATH, OR BURIAL. SHE WAS **GONE** LONG BEFORE I KNEW ANYTHING ABOUT IT…"

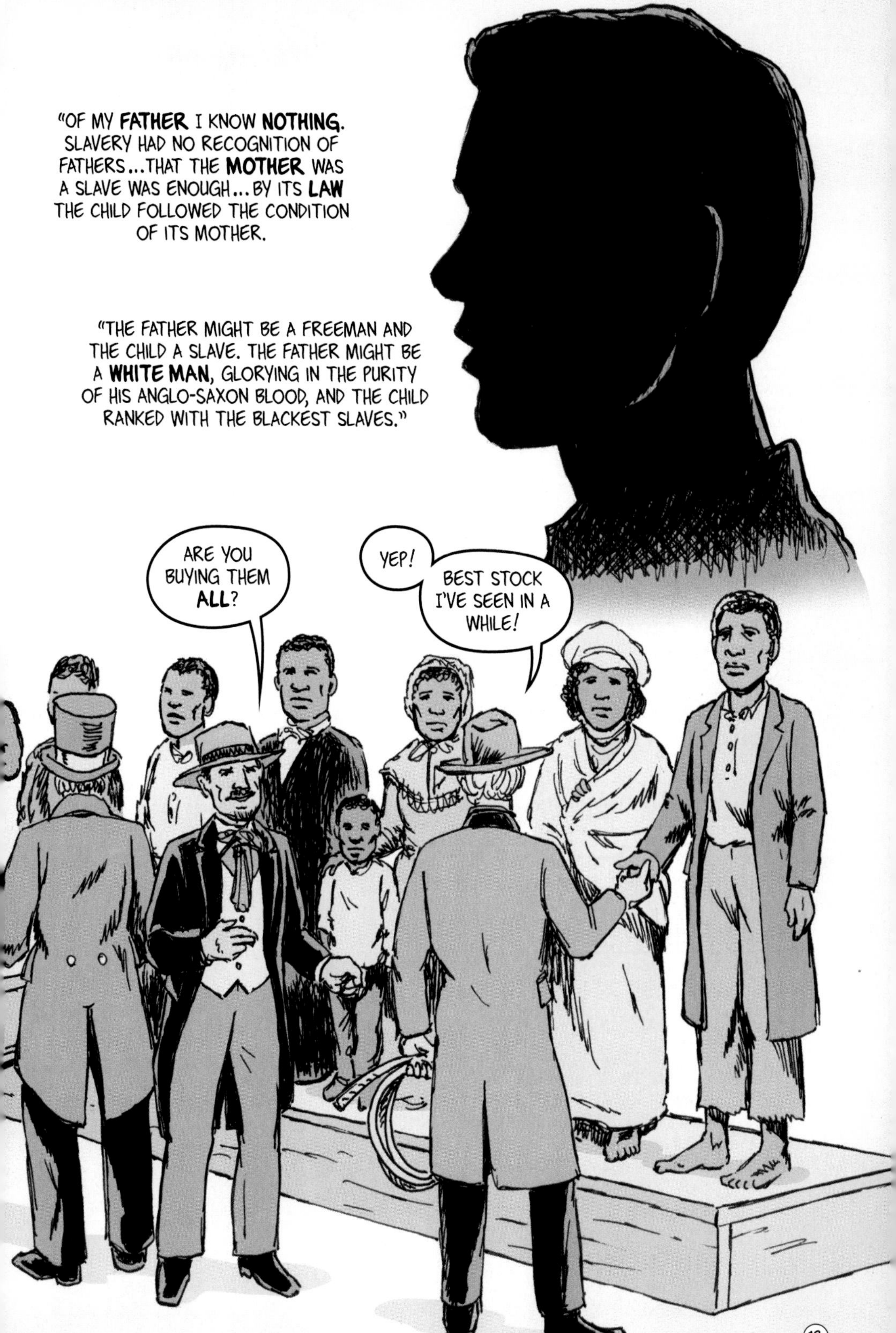
"OF MY FATHER I KNOW NOTHING. SLAVERY HAD NO RECOGNITION OF FATHERS...THAT THE MOTHER WAS A SLAVE WAS ENOUGH...BY ITS LAW THE CHILD FOLLOWED THE CONDITION OF ITS MOTHER.
"THE FATHER MIGHT BE A FREEMAN AND THE CHILD A SLAVE. THE FATHER MIGHT BE A WHITE MAN, GLORYING IN THE PURITY OF HIS ANGLO-SAXON BLOOD, AND THE CHILD RANKED WITH THE BLACKEST SLAVES."
ARE YOU BUYING THEM ALL?
YEP!
BEST STOCK I'VE SEEN IN A WHILE!

FRED BAILEY NOW LIVED IN THE HOME OF HIS NEW MASTER, CAPTAIN
AARON ANTHONY. FRED'S BED WAS THE FLOOR OF A KITCHEN CLOSET.

SHOO, THERE, FREDERICK!

THOUGH CAPTAIN ANTHONY, A WIDOWER, WAS THE **MASTER** OF HIS HOUSE, IT WAS RULED WITH AN IRON HAND BY THE SLAVE CALLED **AUNT KATY** -- "AUNT" BEING A SIGN OF RESPECT.

DOUGLASS WROTE THAT SHE WAS "AMBITIOUS OF OLD MASTER'S FAVOR, ILL-TEMPERED AND **CRUEL** BY NATURE... SHE HAD A **STRONG HOLD** UPON OLD MASTER, FOR SHE WAS A **FIRST-RATE COOK**, AND VERY INDUSTRIOUS."

YES'M.

FOOD'LL BE READY ALL IN GOOD TIME!

FREDERICK! DON'T GET GRABBY! OTHERS GOTTA EAT!

OWW!

HAW!

THE CHILDREN ATE FROM A **WOODEN TROUGH**, "LIKE SO MANY PIGS." DOUGLASS REMEMBERED, "HE THAT ATE FASTEST GOT MOST."

BUT I HARDLY GOT **ANYTHING**!

BUT AUNT KATY TOOK A **DISLIKE** TO FRED. HE RECALLED THAT "WANT OF FOOD WAS MY CHIEF TROUBLE DURING MY FIRST SUMMER."

IN ONE OF HER RARE VISITS TO THE MANSION, FRED'S MOTHER DISCOVERED THAT AUNT KATY WAS STARVING HER SON. SHE IMMEDIATELY MADE A LARGE GINGER CAKE FOR HIM AND, DOUGLASS RECALLED, "READ AUNT KATY A LECTURE WHICH WAS NEVER FORGOTTEN."

YOU DON'T STARVE MY SON!

IT WAS ALSO THE NIGHT WHEN HE LEARNED "THAT I WAS NOT ONLY A CHILD, BUT **SOMEBODY'S** CHILD. I WAS GRANDER UPON MY MOTHER'S KNEE THAN A KING UPON HIS THRONE."

MY FREDERICK HAS JUST AS MUCH RIGHT TO FOOD AS THE **OTHER** CHILDREN!

"BUT MY TRIUMPH WAS SHORT," HE WROTE. THE NEXT MORNING FRED AWOKE "TO FIND MY MOTHER GONE AND MYSELF AT THE MERCY AGAIN OF THE **VIRAGO** IN MY MASTER'S KITCHEN, WHOSE FIERY WRATH WAS MY CONSTANT DREAD."

YOU GET **UPPITY** ON ME, FREDERICK, AN' YOU'LL **PAY!**

YES'M.

15

CAPTAIN ANTHONY OWNED ABOUT 200 ACRES AND ABOUT **30 SLAVES**.
HE HOPED TO OWN MORE LAND, AND MANY MORE SLAVES.

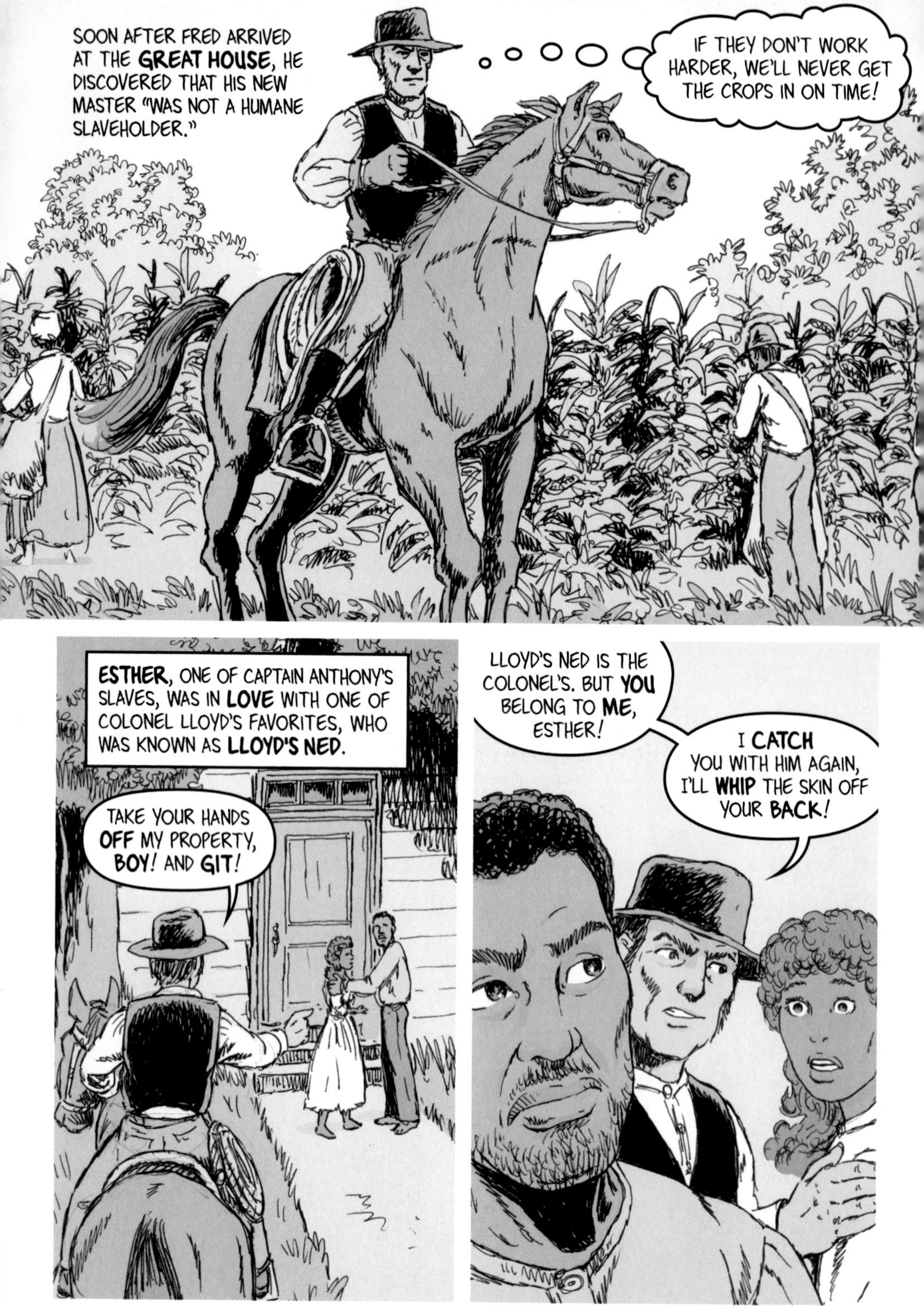
SOON AFTER FRED ARRIVED AT THE **GREAT HOUSE**, HE DISCOVERED THAT HIS NEW MASTER "WAS NOT A HUMANE SLAVEHOLDER."
IF THEY DON'T WORK HARDER, WE'LL NEVER GET THE CROPS IN ON TIME!
ESTHER, ONE OF CAPTAIN ANTHONY'S SLAVES, WAS IN **LOVE** WITH ONE OF COLONEL LLOYD'S FAVORITES, WHO WAS KNOWN AS **LLOYD'S NED**.
TAKE YOUR HANDS **OFF** MY PROPERTY, **BOY**! AND **GIT**!
LLOYD'S NED IS THE COLONEL'S. BUT **YOU** BELONG TO **ME**, ESTHER!
I **CATCH** YOU WITH HIM AGAIN, I'LL **WHIP** THE SKIN OFF YOUR **BACK**!

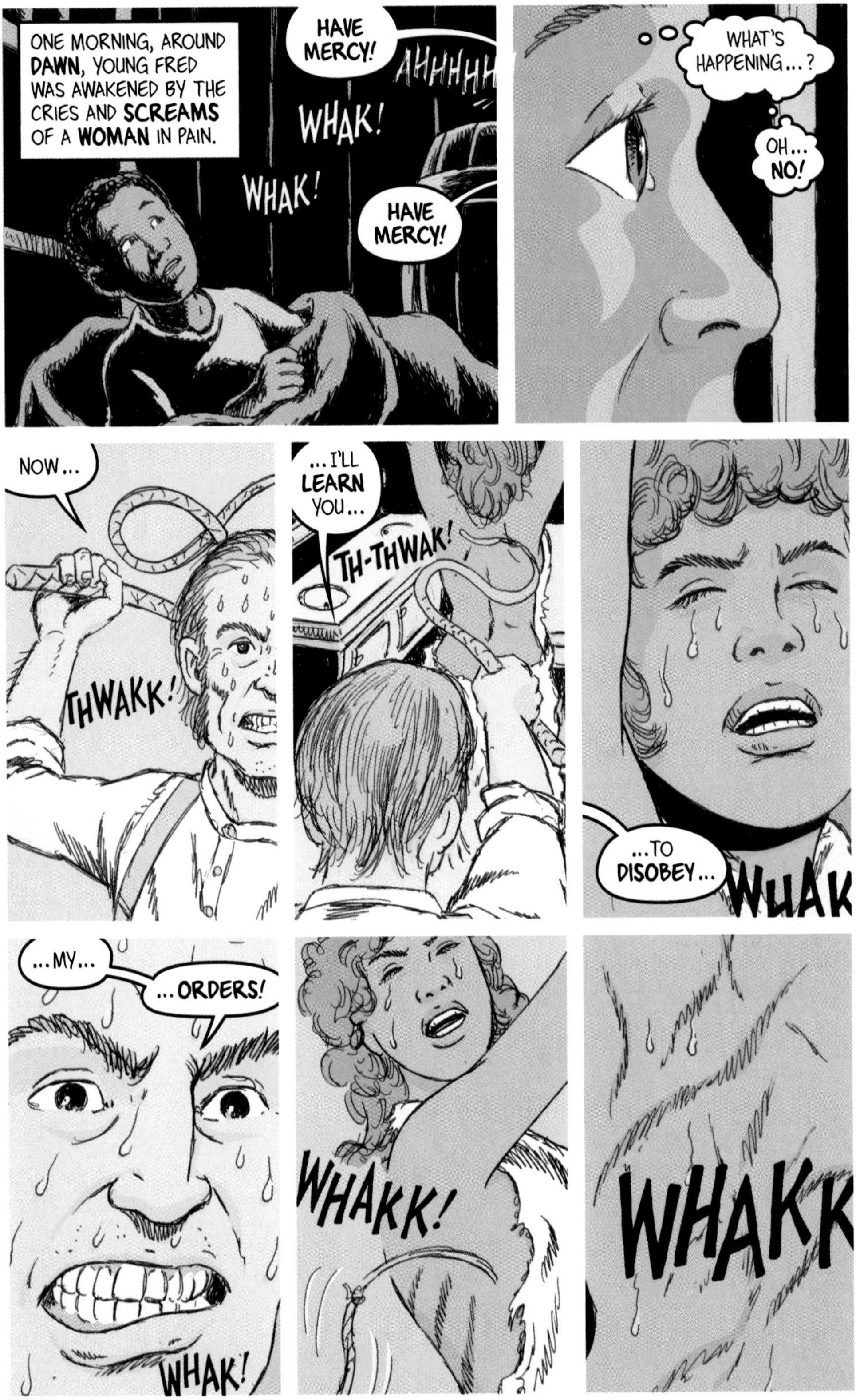
ONE MORNING, AROUND DAWN, YOUNG FRED WAS AWAKENED BY THE CRIES AND SCREAMS OF A WOMAN IN PAIN.
HAVE MERCY!
AHHHHH
WHAK!
WHAK!
HAVE MERCY!
WHAT'S HAPPENING...?
OH... NO!
NOW...
THWAKK!
...I'LL LEARN YOU...
TH-THWAK!
...TO DISOBEY...
WHAK
...MY...
...ORDERS!
WHAK!
WHAKK!
WHAKK

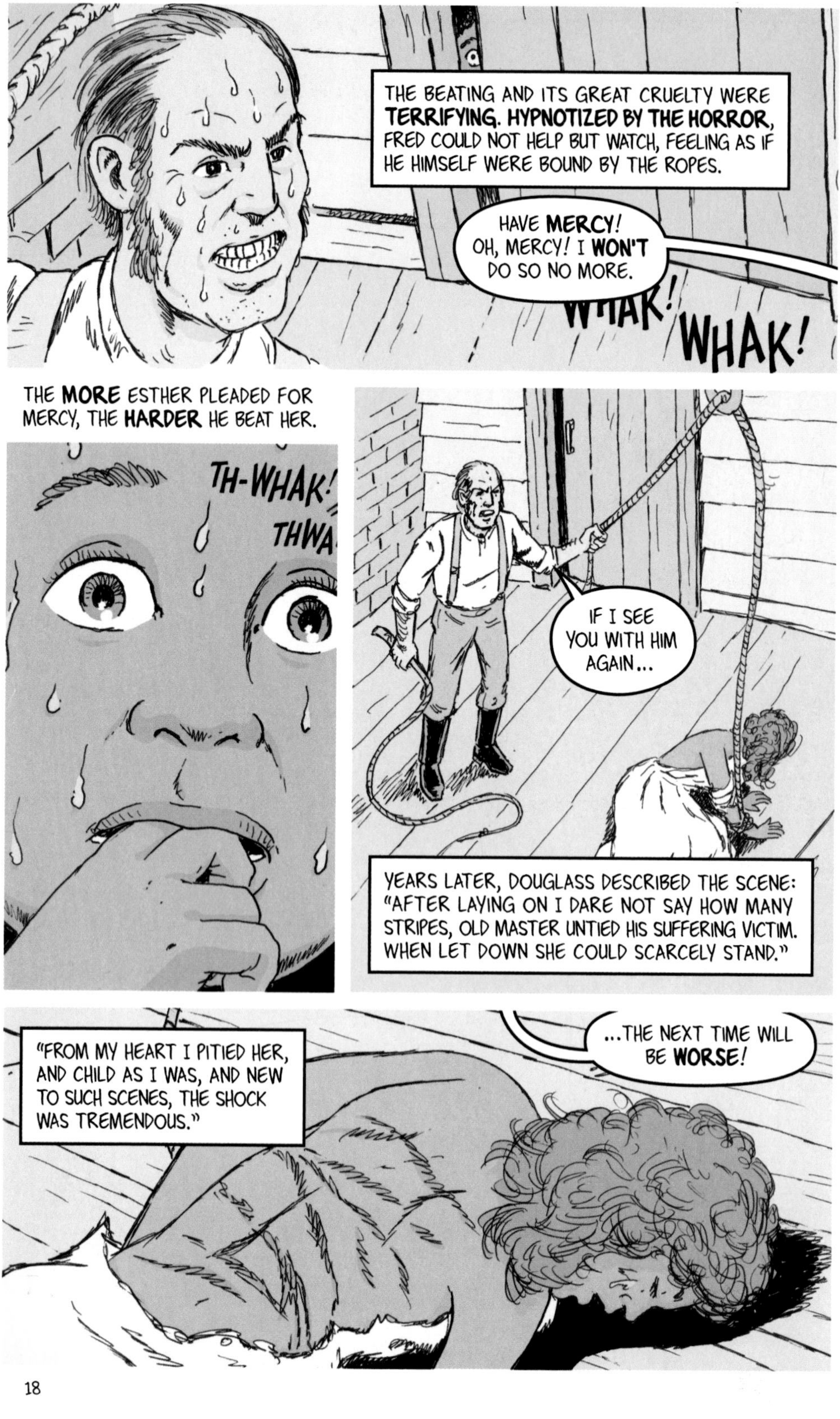

THE BEATING AND ITS GREAT CRUELTY WERE **TERRIFYING. HYPNOTIZED BY THE HORROR,** FRED COULD NOT HELP BUT WATCH, FEELING AS IF HE HIMSELF WERE BOUND BY THE ROPES.
HAVE **MERCY**! OH, MERCY! I **WON'T** DO SO NO MORE.
WHAK!
WHAK!
THE **MORE** ESTHER PLEADED FOR MERCY, THE **HARDER** HE BEAT HER.
TH-WHAK!
THWA
IF I SEE YOU WITH HIM AGAIN...
YEARS LATER, DOUGLASS DESCRIBED THE SCENE: "AFTER LAYING ON I DARE NOT SAY HOW MANY STRIPES, OLD MASTER UNTIED HIS SUFFERING VICTIM. WHEN LET DOWN SHE COULD SCARCELY STAND."
"FROM MY HEART I PITIED HER, AND CHILD AS I WAS, AND NEW TO SUCH SCENES, THE SHOCK WAS TREMENDOUS."
...THE NEXT TIME WILL BE **WORSE**!

BUT FRED BAILEY'S LIFE AT THE GREAT HOUSE WAS NOT MARKED ONLY BY FEAR AND VIOLENCE.

OVER TIME, HE BECAME A **COMPANION** AND PLAYMATE TO COLONEL LLOYD'S YOUNGEST SON, **DANIEL**.

GOOD SHOT, MASTER DANIEL!

AS A MEMBER OF THE UPPER GENTRY, DANIEL HAD TO BE **EDUCATED** SO HE COULD TAKE HIS PROPER PLACE IN SOCIETY. THIS BECAME THE TASK OF A TUTOR FROM MASSACHUSETTS, **JOEL PAGE**.

IN ADDITION TO THE THREE Rs, PAGE TAUGHT YOUNG DANIEL **DICTION**. IT WOULDN'T DO FOR A FUTURE MASTER TO SPEAK "COUNTRY" -- WHICH IS TO SAY, LIKE A **PLANTATION SLAVE**.

NOW, REPEAT AFTER ME: I CAN...

AH KIN --

NO. "I CAN..."

EARLY ON, FRED BAILEY DEMONSTRATED THE TALENT TO **MIMIC** ANIMALS AND EVEN PEOPLE'S VOICES. HE HAD ABOVE-AVERAGE **INTELLIGENCE**, CURIOSITY, AND A HUNGER TO KNOW THINGS.

I CAN...

HE DISCOVERED THAT IF YOU SOUNDED "**CULTURED**," PEOPLE LOOKED AT YOU DIFFERENTLY. THOUGH NOT ALLOWED TO READ OR WRITE, HE COULD LISTEN. AND HE LEARNED, ALTHOUGH HE KEPT IT TO HIMSELF.

FRED WAS ABOUT 12 YEARS OLD NOW.

IN 1826, TWO YEARS AFTER FRED BAILEY HAD ARRIVED AT WYE HOUSE, HE FOUND HIS LIFE **UPROOTED** AGAIN. CAPTAIN ANTHONY'S HEALTH WAS FAILING. THIS CAUSED A **SHUFFLING** OF FAMILY CIRCUMSTANCES.

NOW, Y'ALL BE CAREFUL, THERE!

CAPTAIN ANTHONY'S DAUGHTER, **LUCRETIA**, AND HER HUSBAND, **THOMAS AULD**, SUPERVISED THE APPORTIONING OF THE CAPTAIN'S **PROPERTY** -- WHICH, OF COURSE, INCLUDED HIS SLAVES.

BYE!

BYE, LUCRETIA!

THOMAS HAS A BROTHER, **HUGH**, WHO LIVES IN **BALTIMORE**. YOU WILL BE SENT THERE.

DON'T WORRY, FRED. HUGH'S WIFE, **SOPHIA**, IS A **KIND** MISTRESS.

FRED **WAS** WORRIED. HE WAS LEAVING **PLANTATION LIFE** BEHIND TO LIVE IN A HOUSE IN A **CITY** FOR THE FIRST TIME. LUCRETIA AULD CLEANED HIM UP AND GAVE FRED HIS VERY FIRST PAIR OF **PANTS**.

LUCRETIA PLACED FRED IN THE CARE OF HIS COUSIN **TOM**, A CABIN-BOY SLAVE ON THE CREW OF THE *SALLY LLOYD*. THIS WAS ONE OF COLONEL LLOYD'S **SHIPS** THAT SAILED THE ROUTE FROM WYE HOUSE TO BALTIMORE.

Y'ALL ARE GOING TO **LOVE** BALTIMORE, FRED.

YOU SURE?

YEP!

THOUGH HE EXPERIENCED A NATURAL FEAR OF THE **UNKNOWN**, FRED WAS NOT SAD TO LEAVE THE WYE HOUSE PLANTATION, WHERE HE HAD LEARNED THE CRUEL DIFFERENCE BETWEEN **MASTER** AND **SLAVE**.

TOM TOLD HIM OF THE MANY GREAT **WONDERS** TO BE SEEN IN BALTIMORE.

STILL SCARED, FREDDY?

NOT SO MUCH AS BEFORE.

OF THAT DAY, FRED LATER WROTE: "I...GAVE TO COLONEL LLOYD'S PLANTATION WHAT I HOPED WOULD BE THE LAST LOOK I SHOULD GIVE TO IT, OR TO ANY *PLACE LIKE IT*...I...SPENT THE REMAINDER OF THE DAY IN LOOKING AHEAD."

TWO DAYS LATER, THE *SALLY LLOYD* ARRIVED AT BALTIMORE.

STAY CLOSE, LITTLE FREDERICK. BALTIMORE'S A **BIG TOWN**. I DON'T WANT TO **LOSE** YOU.

YES, SIR.

NOW FRED WAS TAKEN BY ANOTHER OF THE SHIP'S CREW TO THE HOME AND FAMILY OF HIS **NEW MASTER**, HUGH AULD.

THE AULD HOME WAS ON ALLICIANA STREET, NEAR THE SHIPYARD. FRED WAS MET AT THE DOOR BY **HUGH** AND **SOPHIA AULD** AND THEIR TWO-YEAR-OLD SON, **THOMAS**.

TOMMY, THIS IS YOUR **FREDDY**. FREDDY WILL TAKE CARE OF YOU.

FREDDY, YOU BE **KIND** TO LITTLE TOMMY.

FRED HARDLY NEEDED SOPHIA'S **INSTRUCTION**, FOR HE HAD TAKEN TO THE CHILD ALMOST IMMEDIATELY.

YAY!

AS FOR SOPHIA AULD, DOUGLASS WROTE: "I... SOON CAME TO REGARD HER AS SOMETHING MORE AKIN TO A MOTHER THAN A SLAVEHOLDING MISTRESS."

I LIKE FRED, MAMA.

WE ALL LIKE OUR FREDDY, DEAR.

BUT A LITTLE OVER A YEAR LATER, FRED WAS ONCE AGAIN CRUELLY REMINDED THAT HE WAS A **SLAVE** AND NOT A MEMBER OF THE FAMILY.

HE ABRUPTLY FOUND HIMSELF ABOARD A SHIP, **RETURNING** TO WYE HOUSE.

IN 1826, CAPTAIN AARON ANTHONY **DIED** WITHOUT LEAVING A **WILL**.

THIS MEANT THAT ALL OF HIS **PROPERTY** WOULD BE DIVIDED EQUALLY AMONG HIS THREE CHILDREN, **LUCRETIA**, **ANDREW**, AND **RICHARD**. BUT LUCRETIA DIED BEFORE THE ESTATE WAS SETTLED, AND HER SHARE WENT TO HER **HUSBAND**, THOMAS AULD.

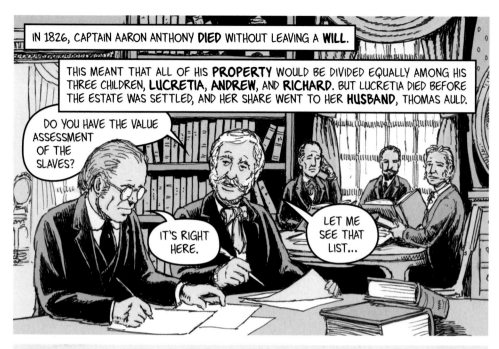

DO YOU HAVE THE VALUE ASSESSMENT OF THE SLAVES?

IT'S RIGHT HERE.

LET ME SEE THAT LIST...

SLAVES WERE PROPERTY.

THAT MEANT THE BAILEY SLAVE FAMILY WAS GOING TO BE SPLIT AMONG THE CAPTAIN'S HEIRS ALONG WITH THE LIVESTOCK, WAGONS, AND FURNITURE.

ANDREW ANTHONY -- A NOTORIOUS **DRUNK** -- WAS GIVEN BETSEY BAILEY, FRED'S GRAND-MOTHER, AND FOUR OF HER GRANDDAUGHTERS. **RICHARD ANTHONY**, LITTLE BETTER THAN HIS BROTHER, GOT AUNT KATY AND HER FAMILY.

Y'ALL ARE **MINE** NOW.

THOMAS AULD WAS GIVEN ONE OF FRED'S AUNTS AND FOUR OF HER CHILDREN. IN ADDITION, THOMAS GOT **FRED** AND HIS SISTER ELIZA.

Y'ALL COME WITH ME.

A FEW DAYS LATER, FRED FOUND HIMSELF **BACK** AT THE HOME OF HUGH AULD. THIS TIME HE WOULD LIVE THERE FOR FIVE AND A HALF YEARS.

BECAUSE OF SOPHIA'S **KINDNESS**, FRED DID NOT HAVE TO HIDE HIS **FASCINATION** WITH WHAT HE CALLED "THIS MYSTERY OF READING."

A DEVOUT METHODIST, SOPHIA REGULARLY READ THE **BIBLE** TO HER SON, TOMMY. FRED'S EYES CONSTANTLY WENT FROM THE PAGE TO HER MOUTH AND BACK AGAIN.

"PURE RELIGION AND UNDEFILED BEFORE GOD AND THE FATHER IS THIS, TO VISIT THE FATHERLESS AND WIDOWS IN THEIR AFFLICTION, AND TO KEEP HIMSELF UNSPOTTED FROM THE WORLD."

MIZ SOPHIA... I'D LIKE TO KNOW HOW TO READ. COULD...DO YOU THINK YOU COULD TEACH ME, MA'AM?

...I WILL, FRED. I'LL TEACH YOU HOW TO READ THE BIBLE.

SOPHIA AULD MUST HAVE THOUGHT IT WAS THE GOOD, CHRISTIAN THING TO DO. BUT HER DECISION HAD **ENORMOUS CONSEQUENCES**, AND FRED'S LIFE WOULD CHANGE **FOREVER**.

WE'LL START WITH THE VERSE I JUST READ TO YOU.

THANK YOU, MA'AM!

PROUD OF HER EFFORTS, ONE DAY SOPHIA ARRANGED A **DEMONSTRATION** FOR HER HUSBAND.

"PURE RELIGION AND UNDEFILED BEFORE GOD AND THE FATHER IS THIS, TO VISIT --"

BUT INSTEAD OF BEING PROUD, HUGH AULD WAS **FURIOUS.**

IF HE LEARNS TO **READ** THE BIBLE, IT WILL FOREVER **UNFIT** HIM TO BE A **SLAVE!** HE SHOULD KNOW NOTHING BUT THE WILL OF HIS **MASTER**, AND LEARN TO **OBEY** IT.

IF YOU TEACH HIM HOW TO READ, HE'LL WANT TO KNOW HOW TO **WRITE**; AND, THIS ACCOMPLISHED, HE'LL BE RUNNING AWAY WITH HIMSELF.

IT WOULD ONLY DO HIM A GREAT DEAL OF HARM.

LATER, DOUGLASS WROTE: "THE **EFFECT** OF HIS WORDS ON ME WAS NEITHER SLIGHT NOR TRANSITORY. HIS IRON SENTENCES, COLD AND HARSH, SUNK LIKE HEAVY WEIGHTS DEEP INTO MY HEART...

"...AND STIRRED UP WITHIN ME A **RE-BELLION** NOT SOON TO BE ALLAYED."

YOU ARE **WRONG** TO DO THIS, MASTER.

I'LL TEACH MYSELF HOW TO READ -- **AND** WRITE!

AND IF **KNOWLEDGE** UNFITS A CHILD TO BE A **SLAVE**...THEN I'LL BE THE MOST **UNFIT SLAVE** IN BALTIMORE!

WHENEVER POSSIBLE, FRED SECRETLY **OBSERVED** HOW PEOPLE WROTE, AND WORKED TO LINK THE SHAPES OF THE LETTERS AND WORDS TO THE SOUNDS HE HEARD.

HE **TAUGHT HIMSELF** TO READ AND WRITE. IN THE PROCESS, FRED LEARNED ABOUT A MOVEMENT CREATED TO FREE THE SLAVES, CALLED **ABOLITION**. HE DISCOVERED THAT THERE WERE PEOPLE IN THE NORTH -- WHITE PEOPLE! -- WHO WERE DEDICATED TO **ABOLISHING SLAVERY**.

HIS HEART TOOK A LEAP.

IN **1828**, THOMAS LINCOLN HIRED ABRAHAM OUT TO LOCAL STORE OWNER JAMES GENTRY TO HELP HIS SON, ALLEN, TAKE A **FLATBOAT** OF GOODS TO **NEW ORLEANS**. THE 2,400-MILE ROUND-TRIP WOULD TAKE ABOUT THREE MONTHS. THE WAGE WAS $8 A MONTH, TO BE PAID TO YOUNG LINCOLN'S **FATHER**.

READY, ABRAHAM?

I SURE AM, ALLEN!

RIVER TRAVEL WAS **DANGEROUS**. THE RIVER COULD BE TREACHEROUS, WITH FAST CURRENTS, WHIRLPOOLS, HIDDEN SANDBARS, AND HALF-SUBMERGED TREES.

LOOK OUT FOR THAT LOG!

LET'S GET HER BACK TO THE MIDDLE...IT'S TOO SHALLOW HERE.

ONE NIGHT, BELOW BATON ROUGE, LOUISIANA, ABE AND ALLEN ANCHORED THEIR FLATBOAT TO A TREE, PLANNING TO RESUME THEIR JOURNEY SOUTH IN THE MORNING.

I'VE NEVER BEEN IN A CITY AS BIG AS NEW ORLEANS. HAVE YOU, ABRAHAM?

NOPE.

THAT NIGHT, SEVEN NEGROES CREPT ABOARD, INTENDING TO ROB THE FLATBOAT.

GIT 'EM!

LOOK OUT, ALLEN!

OUTNUMBERED AND **UNARMED**, THE DESPERATE ALLEN DECIDED TO TRY A **BLUFF** AS HE BEGAN CUTTING THE ANCHOR ROPE.

LINCOLN! GET THE **GUNS** AND **SHOOT**!

THE BLUFF **WORKED**, AND THE ROBBERS RUSHED BACK ASHORE AS THE BOAT DRIFTED DOWN THE RIVER.

A FEW DAYS LATER, ALLEN AND ABE ARRIVED IN **NEW ORLEANS**. IT WAS THE **FIRST TIME** EITHER HAD COME INTO CLOSE CONTACT WITH **SLAVE CULTURE**.

WHAT THEY SAW WAS GRIM.

HIS FAMILY'S RELIGION PREACHED AGAINST SLAVERY, AS DID THE BOOKS ABE HAD READ. AND THE WAY HIS FATHER TREATED HIM -- HIRING HIM OUT AS A LABORER AND KEEPING THE PAY FOR HIMSELF -- MADE YOUNG LINCOLN **REJECT** BOTH THE IDEA AND THE REALITY OF **SLAVERY**.

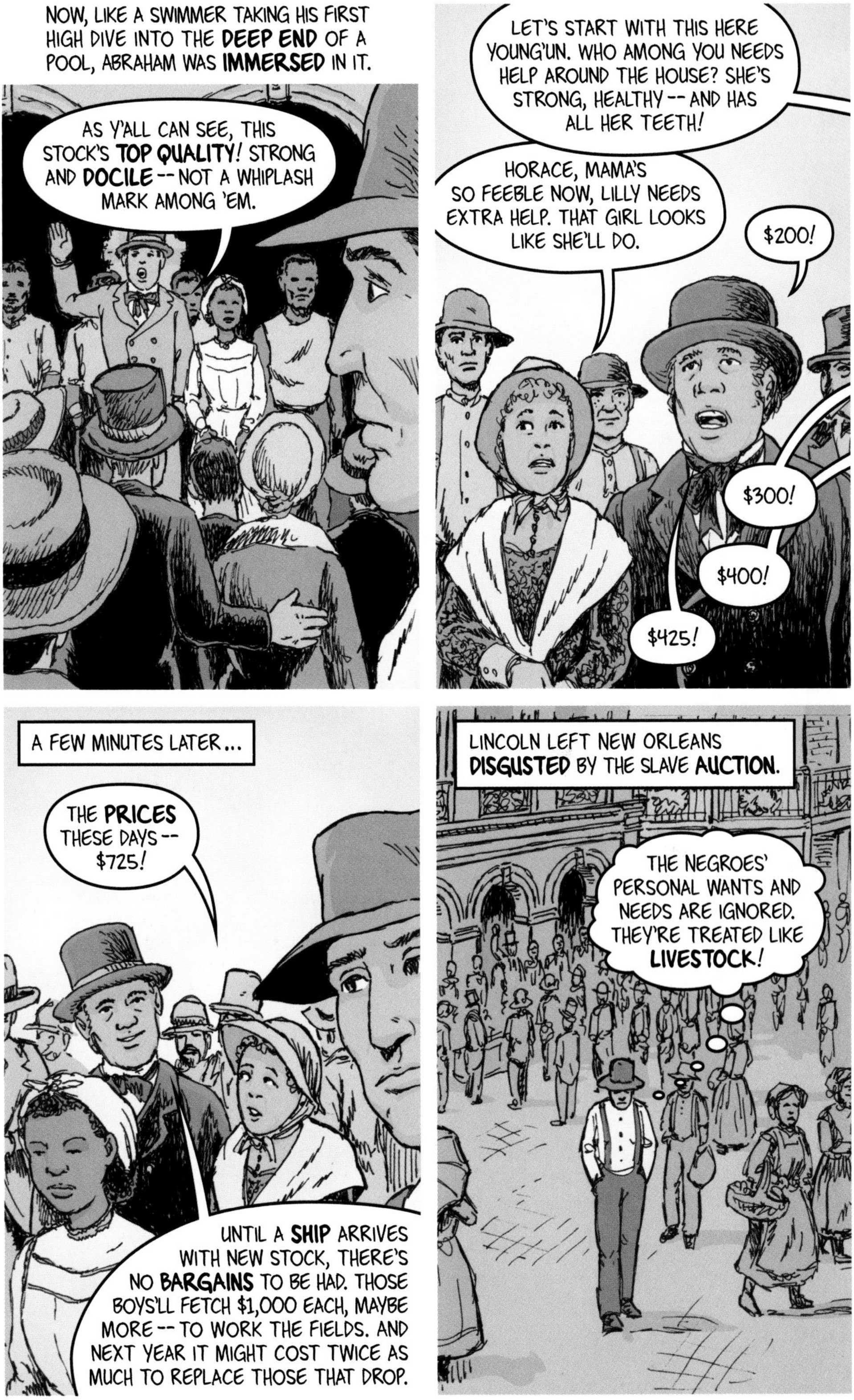

NOW, LIKE A SWIMMER TAKING HIS FIRST HIGH DIVE INTO THE **DEEP END** OF A POOL, ABRAHAM WAS **IMMERSED** IN IT.
AS Y'ALL CAN SEE, THIS STOCK'S **TOP QUALITY**! STRONG AND **DOCILE** -- NOT A WHIPLASH MARK AMONG 'EM.
LET'S START WITH THIS HERE YOUNG'UN. WHO AMONG YOU NEEDS HELP AROUND THE HOUSE? SHE'S STRONG, HEALTHY -- AND HAS ALL HER TEETH!
HORACE, MAMA'S SO FEEBLE NOW, LILLY NEEDS EXTRA HELP. THAT GIRL LOOKS LIKE SHE'LL DO.
$200!
$300!
$400!
$425!
A FEW MINUTES LATER...
THE **PRICES** THESE DAYS -- $725!
UNTIL A **SHIP** ARRIVES WITH NEW STOCK, THERE'S NO **BARGAINS** TO BE HAD. THOSE BOYS'LL FETCH $1,000 EACH, MAYBE MORE -- TO WORK THE FIELDS. AND NEXT YEAR IT MIGHT COST TWICE AS MUCH TO REPLACE THOSE THAT DROP.
LINCOLN LEFT NEW ORLEANS **DISGUSTED** BY THE SLAVE **AUCTION**.
THE NEGROES' PERSONAL WANTS AND NEEDS ARE IGNORED. THEY'RE TREATED LIKE **LIVESTOCK**!

IN EARLY **1831**, THOMAS LINCOLN AGAIN UPROOTED THE FAMILY AND MOVED NOW TO ILLINOIS. THEY HOMESTEADED ALONG THE **SANGAMON RIVER** NEAR DECATUR.

THERE'S OUR NEW HOME!

IT WAS THE YEAR ABRAHAM TURNED 22.

NOW LEGALLY FREE FROM HIS FATHER'S CONTROL, ABRAHAM HIRED HIMSELF OUT AS A CREW-MAN ON ANOTHER **FLATBOAT TRIP** TO NEW ORLEANS.

THE MONEY I EARN NOW WILL BE **MINE**.

IN THIS **SECOND TRIP** HE WITNESSED VIOLENT **ABUSES** OF SEVERAL SLAVES. THIS **SICKENED** HIM TO SUCH AN EXTENT THAT, 20 YEARS LATER, HE SAID, "THE HORRID PICTURES ARE IN MY MIND YET."

THAT'S SO **CRUEL**. IT'S **INTOLERABLE!**

IN **SEPTEMBER 1831**, HE BE-CAME A CLERK IN A STORE IN **NEW SALEM, ILLINOIS**, AND QUICKLY IMPRESSED EVERYONE WHO CAME IN CONTACT WITH HIM.

HE'S AMONG THE BEST CLERKS I EVER SAW.

SO, MENTOR GRAHAM, IS THIS THE YOUNG MAN YOU'VE BEEN TALKING UP?

YEP. ABRAHAM LINCOLN'S HIS NAME.

LINCOLN, YOU'RE THE MOST POLITE AND HELPFUL CLERK I'VE EVER DONE BUSI-NESS WITH.

WHY, THANK YOU, MR. SULLIVAN.

DISPUTED BETWEEN MAINE AND COLONY OF NEW BRUNSWICK (UK)

DISPUTED BETWEEN MICHIGAN TERRITORY AND RUPERT'S LAND (UK)

NEW HAMPSHIRE

MAINE

VERMONT

UNORGANIZED TERRITORY

MICHIGAN TERRITORY

MASS

NEW YORK

RHODE ISLAND

MICHIGAN TERRITORY

CONNECTICUT

PENNSYLVANIA

NEW JERSEY

ILLINOIS INDIANA OHIO

DELAWARE

DC

MARYLAND

VIRGINIA

(DC = DISTRICT OF COLUMBIA)

MISSOURI

KENTUCKY

NORTH CAROLINA

TENNESSEE

United States of America
1836

DISPUTED BETWEEN MEXICO AND TEXAS

MILLER COUNTY (DISPUTED BETWEEN TEXAS AND ARKANSAS TERRITORY)

ARKANSAS TERRITORY

SOUTH CAROLINA

ALABAMA GEORGIA

REPUBLIC OF TEXAS

MISSISSIPPI

SLAVERY ELSEWHERE IN THE WORLD WAS EITHER IN **DECLINE** OR BEING PEACEFULLY **ABOLISHED** THROUGH LEGISLATION. ONLY THE **UNITED STATES** MOVED TO **INCREASE SLAVERY.** THE REASONS WERE SIMPLE:

MONEY AND **FEAR.**

BY 1831, THE **COTTON GIN** ALLOWED PLANTERS TO EXPAND THE CULTIVATION OF COTTON INLAND, MAKING SLAVERY MORE PROFITABLE THAN EVER. AT THE SAME TIME, SOUTHERN STATES FEARED THAT **WESTWARD EXPANSION** WOULD CREATE NEW STATES OPPOSED TO SLAVERY, COSTING THEM POLITICAL POWER AND POTENTIAL INCOME.

TO **COUNTER** THIS, SOUTHERN LEGISLATORS SUCCESSFULLY PASSED LAWS THROUGH THE FEDERAL GOVERNMENT THAT FAVORED **SLAVERY AND SLAVE OWNERS.** THEY EVEN PASSED "GAG RULES" THAT FOR YEARS PREVENTED THE SUBJECT OF SLAVERY FROM BEING DISCUSSED IN CONGRESS.

BUT THAT COULD NOT STOP ABOLITIONISTS FROM SPEAKING OUT. **WILLIAM LLOYD GARRISON** WAS A LEADING ABOLITIONIST WHOSE NEWSPAPER, *THE LIBERATOR*, ATTACKED SLAVERY AND MADE SOUTHERNERS FEEL DEFENSIVE ABOUT THEIR LABOR SYSTEM. WHEN A SLAVE NAMED **NAT TURNER** LED A SLAVE REVOLT IN VIRGINIA IN 1831, SOUTHERNERS PASSED EVEN MORE RESTRICTIVE SLAVE LAWS.

THESE EVENTS MOVED FREDERICK DOUGLASS TO **ACT**... AND ABRAHAM LINCOLN TO **THINK** HARD AND LONG ABOUT WHAT SHOULD BE DONE TO SET THINGS RIGHT, AND HOW TO DO IT.

TALBOT COUNTY, JANUARY 1, 1834.

I'M GOING TO **ANOTHER MASTER**...

...BECAUSE I'M JUST A **THING** TO THEM.

A **DISPUTE** BETWEEN THE AULD BROTHERS RESULTED IN THE SLAVE FRED BAILEY BEING RETURNED TO THOMAS IN MARCH 1833. THE REUNION STARTED WELL ENOUGH, THEN RAPIDLY **DETERIORATED**. ACCORDING TO HIS MASTER, FRED BAILEY HAD BECOME A **PROBLEM SLAVE**.

SOMETHING TO BE USED, LIKE A **FARM ANIMAL**.

FOR **SOUTHERN SLAVES**, JANUARY 1 WAS A DAY OF SADNESS AND **DREAD**. THEY CALLED IT THE "DAY OF TEARS" AND "THE WEEPING TIME."

IT WAS ON THAT DAY THAT SLAVE FAMILIES WERE **SEPARATED** BY THEIR MASTERS, AND MANY WERE SOLD TO BECOME FIELD HANDS ON **COTTON PLANTATIONS** IN THE DEEP SOUTH. ONCE THERE, THEY WOULD NEVER BE HEARD FROM AGAIN.

THEY DON'T CARE IF I LIKE IT OR NOT, BECAUSE THEY HAVE **POWER** --

SLAVE OWNERS ALSO USED NEW YEAR'S DAY TO SELL OR LEASE "LAZY" OR REBELLIOUS SLAVES. THOMAS AULD DECIDED HE WOULD EARN SOME MONEY BY **LEASING** FRED TO A MAN **SKILLED AT BREAKING THE WILL** OF TROUBLESOME SLAVES.

IN THE **SEVEN-MILE WALK** TO HIS NEW MASTER'S HOUSE, FRED BAILEY HAD MUCH TO THINK ABOUT.

-- AND I DON'T.

FRED'S NEW MASTER WAS **EDWARD COVEY**. NOT BORN TO WEALTH, COVEY WANTED TO GET RICH AS QUICKLY AS POSSIBLE. IN THE LINGO OF THE SLAVES, COVEY WAS A **"STRAINER,"** MEANING HE WAS STRAINING TO ENRICH HIMSELF.

COVEY WAS KNOWN IN THE COUNTY FOR HIS "SKILL" IN **SLAVE DISCIPLINE**. SO LONG AS HE DIDN'T KILL THE SLAVE -- FOR THAT WOULD COST HIM AND THE OWNER MONEY -- COVEY WAS FREE TO **TORTURE** AND BEAT THE SLAVE UNTIL HIS OR HER WILL WAS **BROKEN**.

I WANT THIS FIELD FINISHED BEFORE SUNDOWN, OR THERE'LL BE **HELL** TO PAY!

YES, MASTER COVEY!

SLAVES IN THE COUNTY CALLED HIM **THE SNAKE**.

SO FAR, YOUNG FRED BAILEY HAD LED THE **BEST LIFE** SLAVERY HAD TO OFFER. HE HAD WORKED AS A **DOMESTIC** IN THE GREAT HOUSE AND ITS GROUNDS AND BEEN A COMPANION TO TWO MASTERS' SONS.

NOW HE FOUND HIMSELF AT THE **BOTTOM**, WORKING AS A **FIELD HAND** FOR A MASTER WHOSE MISSION WAS TO CRUSH HIS WILL. THE **BREAKING** BEGAN THREE DAYS AFTER FRED ARRIVED.

C'MERE, BOY!

BUCK'S THE "IN-HAND" OX. DARBY'S THE "OFF-HAND" OX. TO MAKE 'EM STOP, SAY "WHOA!" "GEE" MEANS "FASTER." AND "HITHER" MEANS "COME HERE." REMEMBER THAT, **BOY**!

NOW GO GATHER **WOOD** YONDER PAST THAT STAND OF TREES. SHOULDN'T TAKE YOU LONGER THAN **MID-MORNING**.

YES, MASTER COVEY.

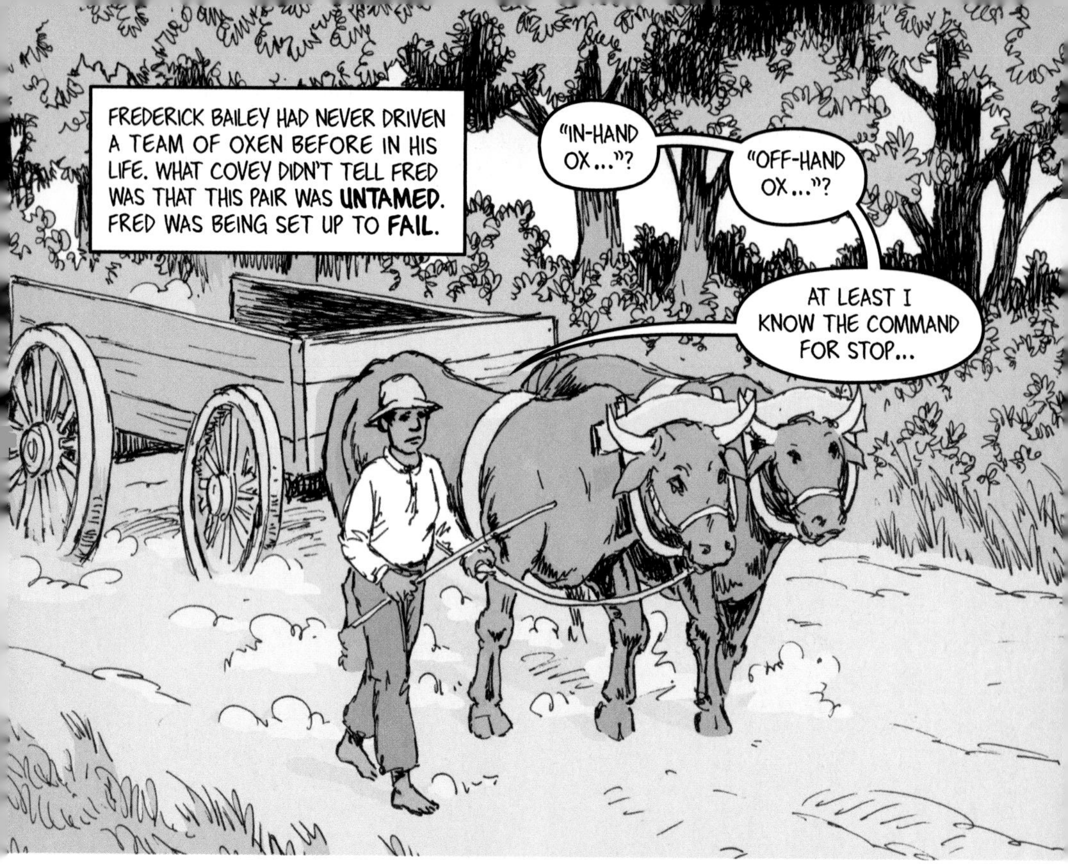
FREDERICK BAILEY HAD NEVER DRIVEN A TEAM OF OXEN BEFORE IN HIS LIFE. WHAT COVEY DIDN'T TELL FRED WAS THAT THIS PAIR WAS **UNTAMED**. FRED WAS BEING SET UP TO **FAIL**.
"IN-HAND OX..."?
"OFF-HAND OX..."?
AT LEAST I KNOW THE COMMAND FOR STOP...

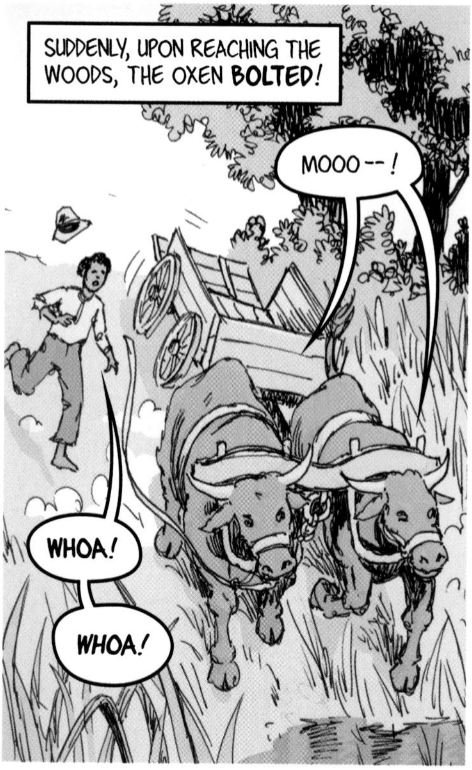
SUDDENLY, UPON REACHING THE WOODS, THE OXEN **BOLTED**!
MOOO--!
WHOA!
WHOA!

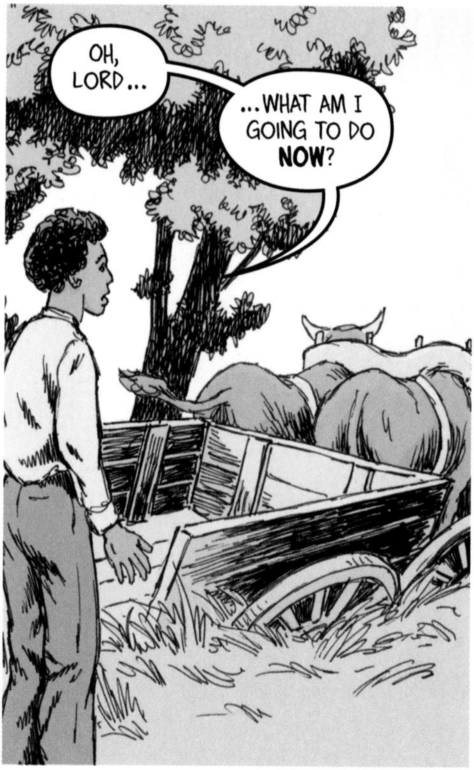
OH, LORD...
...WHAT AM I GOING TO DO **NOW**?

SOMEHOW, FRED MANAGED TO **REPAIR** THE CART AND CONTINUE WITH HIS TASK.

BUT...

IT'S WELL PAST **NOON**!

MASTER COVEY'S GOING TO BE POWERFUL **ANGRY** WITH ME FOR TAKING TOO LONG.

IN THE TWO PREVIOUS DAYS, FRED BAILEY HAD DISCOVERED THAT HIS NEW MASTER WAS STRICT ABOUT THINGS BEING DONE ON TIME. HE HAD SEEN THAT A SLAVE TAKING **TOO LONG** TO DO ANYTHING COULD SUFFER A SEVERE **BEATING**.

MAYBE IF I **EXPLAIN** WHAT HAPPENED, I **WON'T** BE PUNISHED.

OXEN BOLTED, HUH?

WELL, GO **BACK** TO THE WOODS WITH THE CART.

NOW!

FRED QUICKLY **OBEYED**.

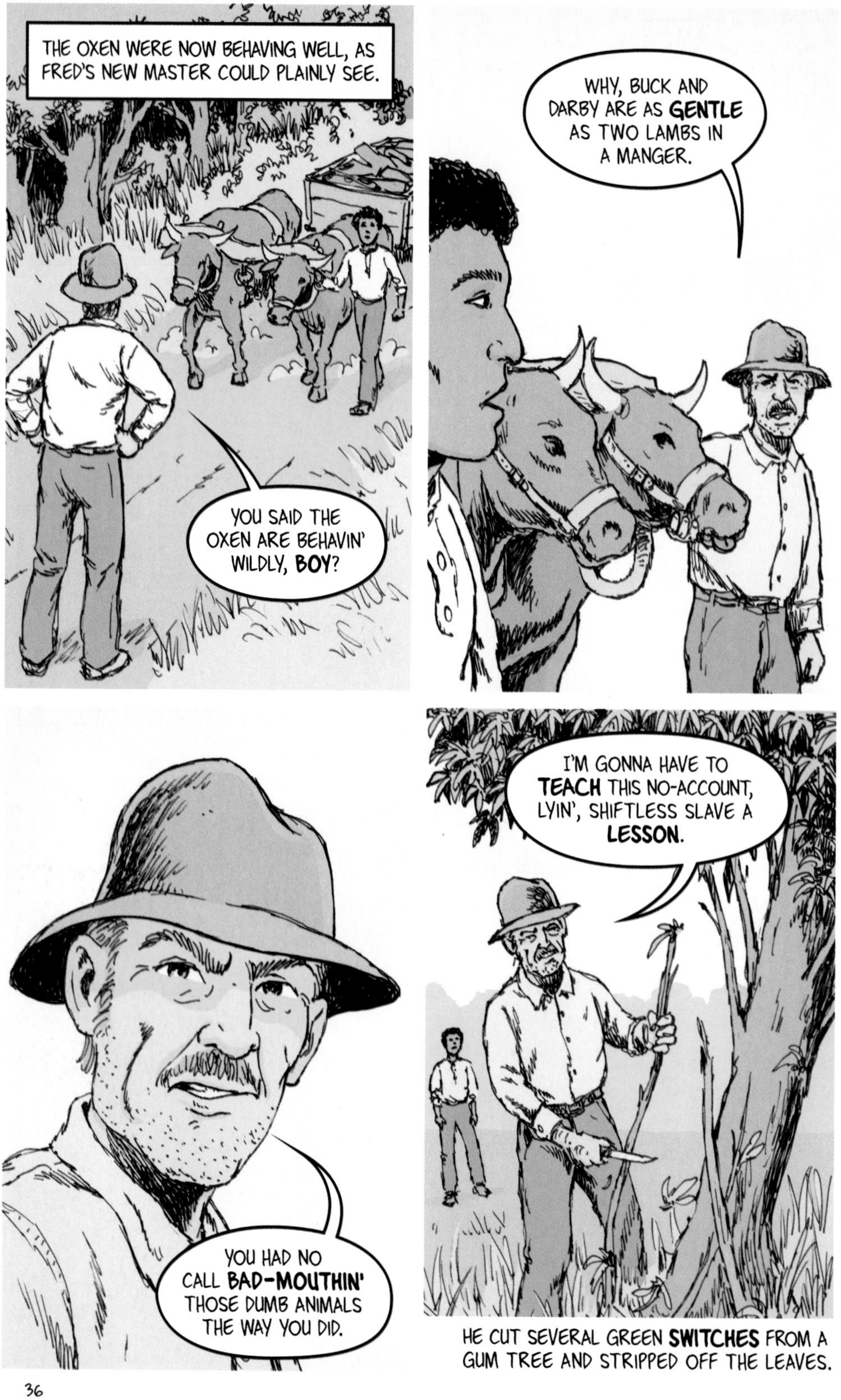
THE OXEN WERE NOW BEHAVING WELL, AS FRED'S NEW MASTER COULD PLAINLY SEE.
YOU SAID THE OXEN ARE BEHAVIN' WILDLY, **BOY**?
WHY, BUCK AND DARBY ARE AS **GENTLE** AS TWO LAMBS IN A MANGER.
YOU HAD NO CALL **BAD-MOUTHIN'** THOSE DUMB ANIMALS THE WAY YOU DID.
I'M GONNA HAVE TO **TEACH** THIS NO-ACCOUNT, LYIN', SHIFTLESS SLAVE A **LESSON**.
HE CUT SEVERAL GREEN **SWITCHES** FROM A GUM TREE AND STRIPPED OFF THE LEAVES.

DOUGLASS LATER WROTE, "THIS WHIPPING WAS THE FIRST OF A NUMBER JUST LIKE IT, AND FOR SIMILAR OFFENSES."

THE **BEATINGS** WOULD **CONTINUE** EVERY WEEK FOR **SIX MONTHS**.

UNABLE TO ENDURE THE BEATINGS ANY LONGER, ONE SATURDAY EVENING FRED BAILEY **RAN AWAY.** HE HAD NOT TRAVELED FAR WHEN HE ENCOUNTERED AN ELDERLY FREEMAN NAMED **SANDY JENKINS.**

JENKINS TOOK FRED TO HIS **HOME.** AFTER LISTENING TO HIS STORY, HE SAID...

GO **BACK** TO MASTER COVEY. BUT **STAND UP** TO HIM. TAKE THESE **ROOTS** -- THEY'RE A CHARM THAT'LL **PROTECT** YOU FROM ANY BEATINGS.

THE NEXT MORNING, FRED DID AS JENKINS INSTRUCTED. AS IT WAS **SUNDAY,** COVEY AND HIS WIFE WENT TO **CHURCH.** FRED WAS NOT **BOTHERED** BY THE MASTER ALL THAT DAY.

ON MONDAY MORNING, FRED WAS IN THE **BARN** WHEN...

I KNOW YOU **RAN AWAY** FROM ME, BOY. AND NOW YOU'RE GOING TO **PAY.**

WHA--?

WHUMP!

UNGH!

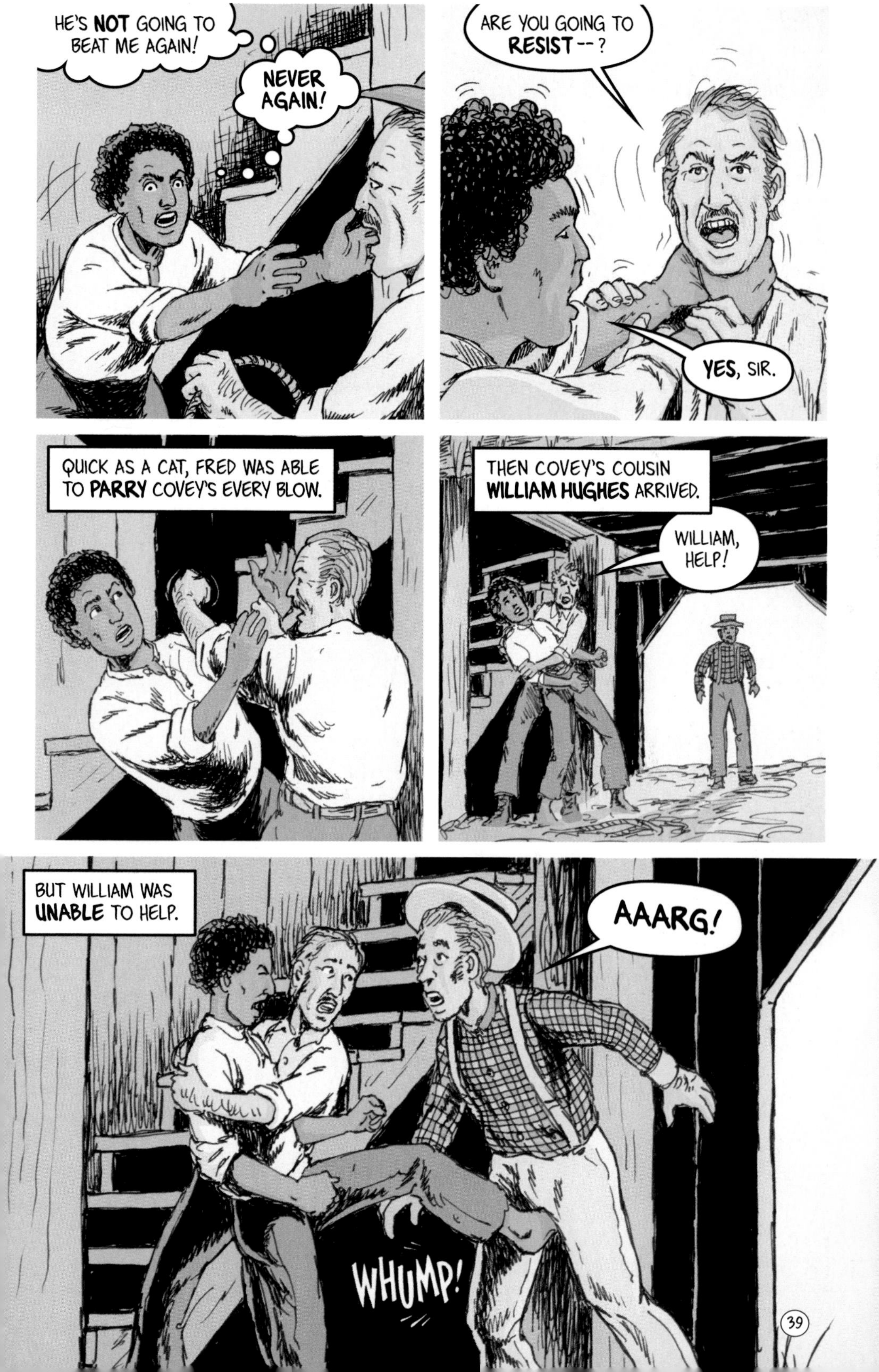
HE'S **NOT** GOING TO BEAT ME AGAIN!
NEVER AGAIN!
ARE YOU GOING TO **RESIST** -- ?
YES, SIR.
QUICK AS A CAT, FRED WAS ABLE TO **PARRY** COVEY'S EVERY BLOW.
THEN COVEY'S COUSIN **WILLIAM HUGHES** ARRIVED.
WILLIAM, HELP!
BUT WILLIAM WAS **UNABLE** TO HELP.
AAARG!
WHUMP!

THEN **BILL SMITH**, A SLAVE COVEY HAD LEASED FROM A NEARBY OWNER, HAPPENED TO WALK BY. COVEY CALLED FOR HIM TO HELP HIM SUBDUE FRED.

BILL!

BILL!

GET OVER HERE AND HELP ME!

BUT SMITH KNEW AND HATED COVEY AND HIS CRUELTY, AND RESPONDED IN THE SLAVES' TIME-HONORED TRADITION OF PLAYING DUMB.

WHAT SHALL I **DO**, MASTER COVEY?

TAKE HOLD OF HIM!

TAKE HOLD OF HIM!

MASTER COVEY, I WANT TO GO TO WORK.

THIS IS YOUR WORK! TAKE HOLD OF HIM!

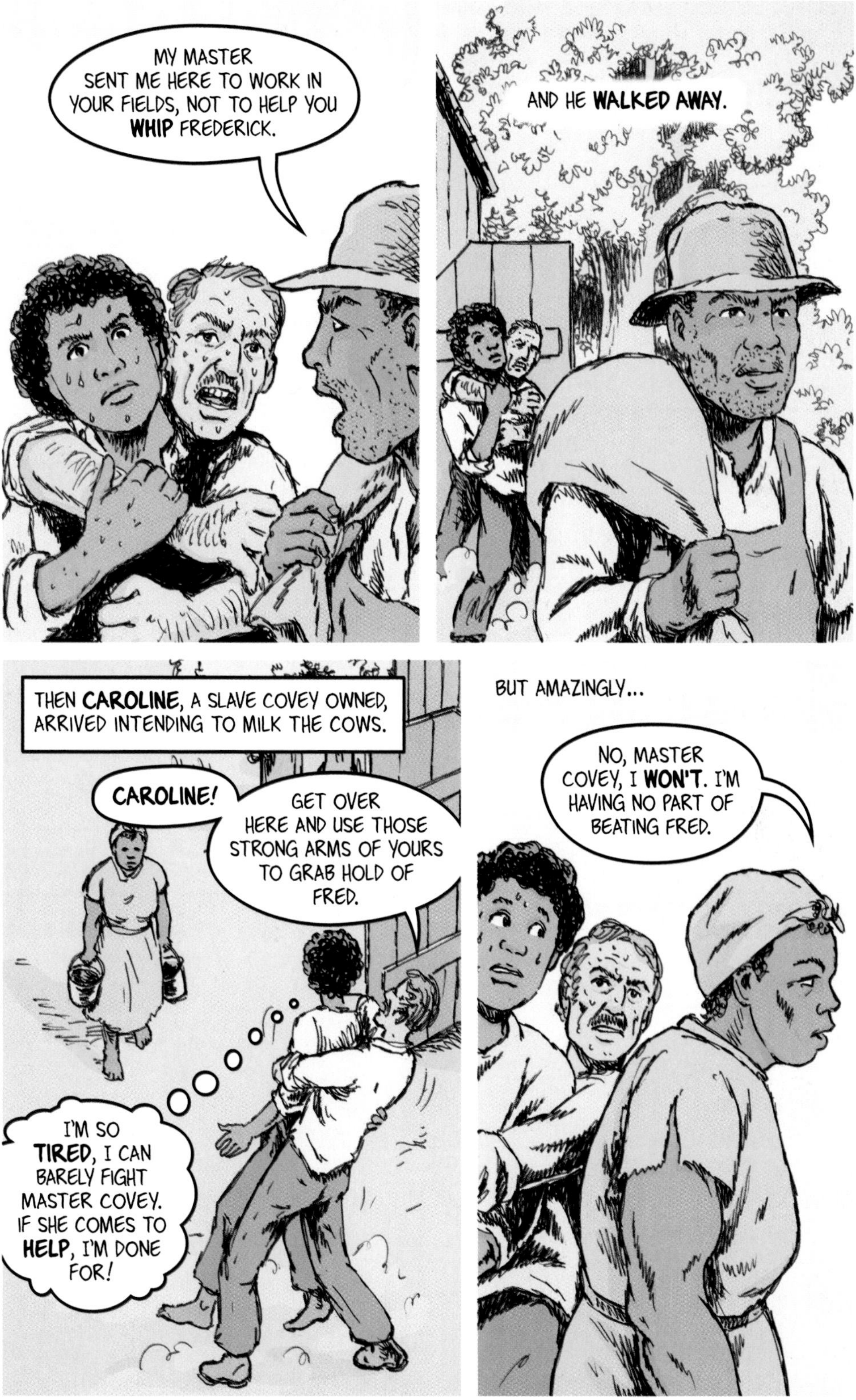

MY MASTER SENT ME HERE TO WORK IN YOUR FIELDS, NOT TO HELP YOU **WHIP** FREDERICK.
AND HE **WALKED AWAY**.
THEN **CAROLINE**, A SLAVE COVEY OWNED, ARRIVED INTENDING TO MILK THE COWS.
CAROLINE!
GET OVER HERE AND USE THOSE STRONG ARMS OF YOURS TO GRAB HOLD OF FRED.
I'M SO **TIRED**, I CAN BARELY FIGHT MASTER COVEY. IF SHE COMES TO **HELP**, I'M DONE FOR!
BUT AMAZINGLY...
NO, MASTER COVEY, I **WON'T**. I'M HAVING NO PART OF BEATING FRED.

FINALLY, THE EXHAUSTED FIGHTERS **RELEASED** EACH OTHER. THE CONFRONTATION WAS **OVER.**

NOW, YOU SCOUNDREL, GO TO YOUR WORK...

...I WOULD NOT HAVE WHIPPED YOU HALF AS HARD IF YOU HAD NOT RESISTED.

COVEY'S WORDS WERE SHEER **BLUSTER,** FOR HE HAD NOT WHIPPED FRED BAILEY AT ALL...NOR WOULD HE EVER AGAIN.

YOUNG FRED HAD **WON!** IT WAS A WATERSHED VICTORY IN HIS LIFE.

BEFORE THIS FIGHT, I WAS... **NOTHING!** NOW...I'M A...**MAN!** AND SOON...I'LL BE A **FREE MAN!**

THE SOUTH DID ALLOW SLAVES TO BECOME FREE THROUGH A PROCESS CALLED **MANUMISSION.** IT HAPPENED ONE OF TWO WAYS. A **MASTER** COULD SET A SLAVE FREE. THIS USUALLY HAPPENED UPON THE **DEATH** OF THE MASTER.

OR THE MASTER COULD ALLOW THE SLAVE TO **EARN MONEY** ON THE SIDE IN ORDER TO **PURCHASE** HIS FREEDOM.

YOU'RE A **FREE MAN,** NOW, JOE!

YESSIR!

BY DECEMBER 1836, FRED HAD BEEN RETURNED TO THOMAS AULD. IF HE WAS **PATIENT,** HE MIGHT EVENTUALLY BE GIVEN, OR BE ABLE TO BUY, HIS FREEDOM.

ONE WAY OR ANOTHER, I'M GOING TO BE FREE!

A THIRD OPTION, **ESCAPE TO THE NORTH,** WAS QUICKER -- AND **DANGEROUS.** FOR THE MOMENT, FRED KNEW HE HAD TO WAIT. BUT HE WOULD NOT WAIT FOREVER.

IN 1836, THOMAS AULD **RETURNED** FRED TO HIS BROTHER, **HUGH**. FRED WAS NOW OLD ENOUGH TO LEARN A TRADE. HUGH, A SHIP'S CAULKER, ARRANGED FOR FRED TO BECOME AN **APPRENTICE**. HE BECAME SKILLED IN THE CRAFT.

THAT'S A FINE JOB, THERE, FREDERICK. YOU'VE GOT THE MAKINGS OF A MASTER CAULKER.

BALTIMORE HAD A LARGE COMMUNITY OF **FREE BLACK PEOPLE**. BECAUSE HUGH AULD ALLOWED FRED FREE TIME ON THE WEEKENDS, HE WAS ABLE TO **SOCIALIZE** WITH MEMBERS OF THAT COMMUNITY.

ONE OF THEM WAS A **FREE WOMAN FIVE YEARS HIS SENIOR**, A DOMESTIC SERVANT NAMED **ANNA MURRAY**.

ANNA, I'D LIKE YOU TO MEET **FREDERICK BAILEY**.

PLEASED TO MEET YOU, MR. BAILEY.

THEY MET AT A LOCAL DEBATING SOCIETY. THOUGH **ILLITERATE**, ANNA COULD READ MUSIC AND WAS AN ACCOMPLISHED **VIOLINIST**. SHE TAUGHT FRED HOW TO PLAY THE VIOLIN, AND THEY OFTEN PERFORMED DUETS.

THEY FELL IN LOVE AND AGREED TO **MARRY**. THEY DECIDED THE WEDDING WOULD NOT HAPPEN IN MARYLAND, WHERE HE WAS A SLAVE, BUT IN THE NORTH... WHERE HE WOULD BE A **FREEMAN**.

FRED WOULD HAVE TO ESCAPE.

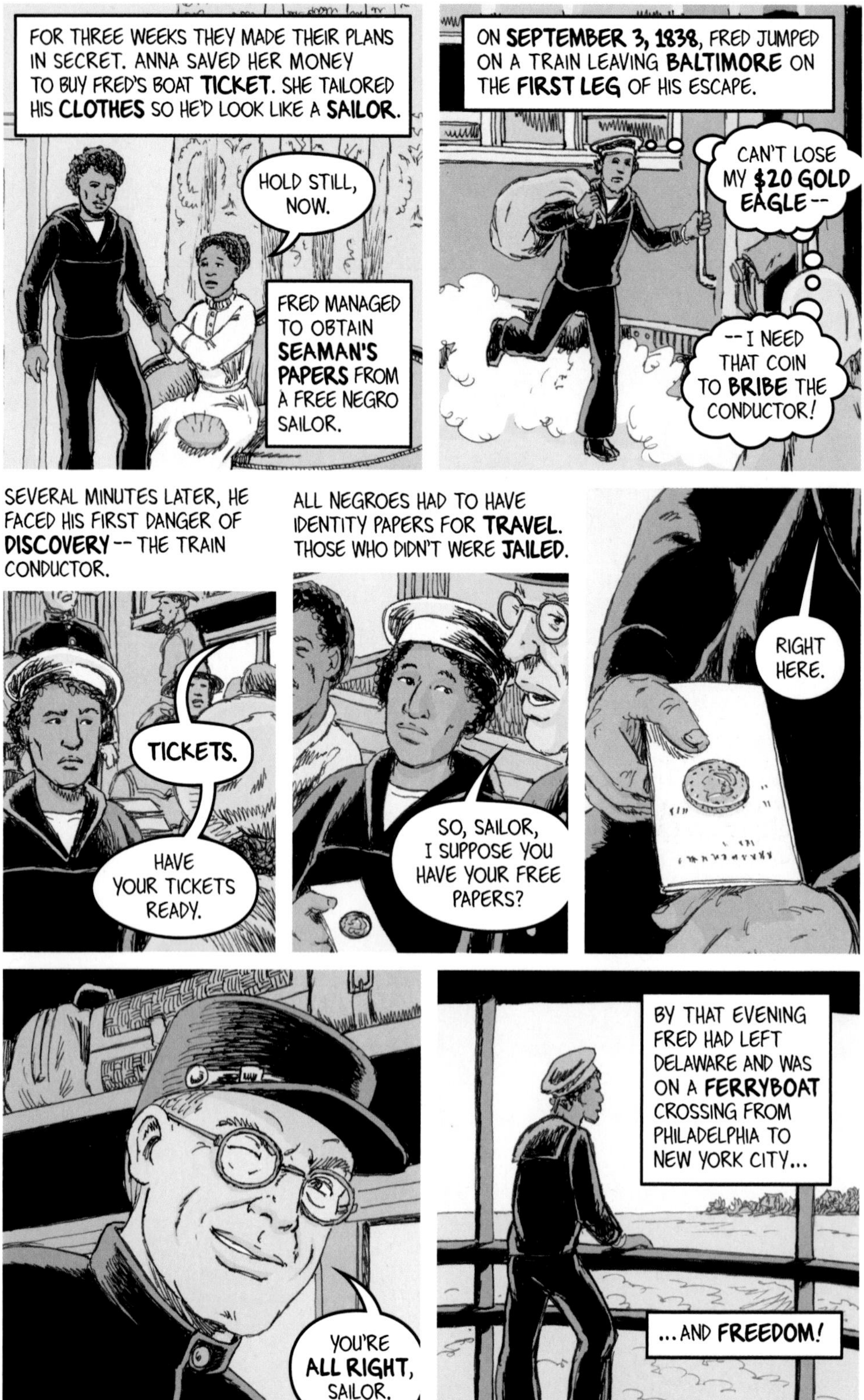
FOR THREE WEEKS THEY MADE THEIR PLANS IN SECRET. ANNA SAVED HER MONEY TO BUY FRED'S BOAT **TICKET**. SHE TAILORED HIS **CLOTHES** SO HE'D LOOK LIKE A **SAILOR**.
HOLD STILL, NOW.
FRED MANAGED TO OBTAIN **SEAMAN'S PAPERS** FROM A FREE NEGRO SAILOR.
ON **SEPTEMBER 3, 1838**, FRED JUMPED ON A TRAIN LEAVING **BALTIMORE** ON THE **FIRST LEG** OF HIS ESCAPE.
CAN'T LOSE MY **$20 GOLD EAGLE**--
--I NEED THAT COIN TO **BRIBE** THE CONDUCTOR!
SEVERAL MINUTES LATER, HE FACED HIS FIRST DANGER OF **DISCOVERY**-- THE TRAIN CONDUCTOR.
TICKETS.
HAVE YOUR TICKETS READY.
ALL NEGROES HAD TO HAVE IDENTITY PAPERS FOR **TRAVEL**. THOSE WHO DIDN'T WERE **JAILED**.
SO, SAILOR, I SUPPOSE YOU HAVE YOUR FREE PAPERS?
RIGHT HERE.
YOU'RE **ALL RIGHT**, SAILOR.
BY THAT EVENING FRED HAD LEFT DELAWARE AND WAS ON A **FERRYBOAT** CROSSING FROM PHILADELPHIA TO NEW YORK CITY...
...AND **FREEDOM**!

SIX YEARS EARLIER. NEW SALEM, ILLINOIS.

I NEED YOUR VOTE, MR. STEWART.

IN **MARCH 1832**, AT THE URGING OF SEVERAL TOWN LEADERS, ABRAHAM LINCOLN ANNOUNCED HIS **CANDIDACY** FOR THE ILLINOIS STATE LEGISLATURE. HE HAD LIVED IN NEW SALEM LESS THAN A YEAR.

IT WAS A **TESTAMENT** TO HOW QUICKLY ABRAHAM HAD GAINED THE **RESPECT** AND ADMIRATION OF HIS **PEERS**.

IT'S YOURS, ABRAHAM. AND I GUARANTEE, YOU HAVE MY NEIGHBORS', TOO!

LINCOLN WAS ONE OF SEVERAL CANDIDATES. THE MOST IMPORTANT LOCAL ISSUES WERE THE ECONOMY, HIGH INTEREST RATES FOR LOANS, AND EDUCATION.

LINCOLN'S OPPONENTS CLAIMED THAT A NEW **RAILROAD** WAS THE PERFECT ANSWER TO IMPROVE TRANSPORTATION AND BOOST LOCAL BUSINESS.

LINCOLN DISAGREED.

YES, A NEW RAILROAD IS EXCITING... BUT IT'S TOO EXPENSIVE.

I SAY THAT CLEARING AND DREDGING THE SHALLOW **SANGAMON RIVER** IS A FASTER AND CHEAPER SOLUTION.

I'VE WORKED ON THE RIVER A LONG TIME, SO I KNOW WHAT HAS TO BE DONE.

TO HELP THE LOCAL ECONOMY, LINCOLN WAS IN FAVOR OF LOWER INTEREST RATES ON LOANS. AND HE SUPPORTED **EDUCATION** PROGRAMS.

EDUCATION IS THE MOST IMPORTANT SUBJECT THAT WE AS A PEOPLE CAN BE ENGAGED IN.

UNLIKE OTHER CANDIDATES WHO EMBELLISHED THEIR PERSONAL STORIES AND SPOKE OF GRAND FUTURES, LINCOLN SPOKE PLAINLY.

I WAS BORN AND HAVE EVER REMAINED IN THE MOST HUMBLE WALKS OF LIFE.

IF ELECTED, HE PROMISED TO **WORK HARD** FOR THE PEOPLE. AND IF HE LOST...

...I AM TOO FAMILIAR WITH DISAPPOINTMENTS TO BE VERY MUCH CHAGRINED.

HIS AUDIENCE **UNDERSTOOD**. HE WAS SAYING THAT HE WAS **JUST LIKE THEM**.

A FEW DAYS LATER, LINCOLN HAD A CHANCE TO BACK HIS WORDS WITH **ACTION**. THE STEAMSHIP *TALISMAN* WAS TRAVELING UP THE SANGAMON AS PART OF A DEMONSTRATION OF THE RIVER'S COMMERCIAL POTENTIAL.

ALONG WITH OTHER LOCAL RESIDENTS, LINCOLN SET TO WORK **CLEARING BRUSH** ALONG THE RIVERBANK AND **PULLING OBSTACLES** OUT OF THE RIVERBED SO THE SHIP COULD EASILY PASS THROUGH.

THEN LINCOLN HELPED **PILOT** THE SHIP ALONG THE 70 MILES OF WATERWAYS HE KNEW.

HARD TO STAR-BOARD. THE CHANNEL'S DEEPEST HERE.

AYE, AYE.

THIS ADVENTURE BOOSTED LINCOLN'S NAME AND **REPUTATION** IN NEW SALEM AND THE REGION.

LINCOLN DID IT!

HE WAS SEEN AS A MAN WHO NOT ONLY KNEW HOW TO TALK PERSUASIVELY BUT ALSO WAS WILLING TO WORK FOR WHAT HE BELIEVED IN.

GOOD DAY, GENTLEMEN!

SIGH

CLOSED FOR BUSNESS

BUT THE **BANKRUPTCY** OF THE STORE WHERE HE WORKED APPEARED TO **STOP** HIS POLITICAL CAREER BEFORE IT COULD START.

THEN, A FEW DAYS LATER, A NEW **DEVELOP-MENT** GAVE HIM ANOTHER **OPPORTUNITY.**

WHAT ARE YOU GOING TO DO, ABRAHAM?

ENLIST!

SAUK INDIAN UPRIS

IT WAS THE OUTBREAK OF THE **BLACK HAWK WAR.**

VOLUNTEERS WERE NEEDED TO HELP THE LOCAL MILITIAS STOP THE INVADING SAUK AND FOX INDIANS, LED BY CHIEF BLACK HAWK. EACH MILITIA HAD A CHANCE TO CHOOSE ITS OWN LEADER.

NOW THAT YOU'RE SWORN IN, GENTLEMEN, YOU MUST CHOOSE YOUR CAPTAIN!

WILLIAM KIRKPATRICK, A LOCAL SAWMILL OWNER, QUICKLY STEPPED FORWARD.

I NOMINATE **MYSELF** FOR THE CAPTAINCY OF THE COMPANY.

A GROUP OF YOUNG MEN WHO WERE LINCOLN'S FRIENDS FROM A NEARBY VILLAGE THEN SPOKE UP.

WE NOMINATE **ABRAHAM LINCOLN.**

MEN VOTED BY ASSEMBLING BEHIND THE MAN THEY WANTED TO LEAD THEM. **LINCOLN** WAS THEIR OVERWHELMING CHOICE BY MORE THAN **TWO** TO ONE. LINCOLN SERVED A TOTAL OF **THREE ENLISTMENTS**, LASTING LESS THAN THREE MONTHS.

AT NO TIME DID HE SEE **COMBAT.** HE LATER SAID, "I WAS OUT OF WORK...AND THERE BEING NO DANGER OF MORE FIGHTING, I COULD DO NOTHING BETTER THAN ENLIST AGAIN."

WE NEED **MORE** ROADS... AND **BETTER** ONES.

BETTER WATERWAYS, TOO.

HIS SERVICE WAS UNEVENTFUL. BUT IT BROUGHT HIM INTO **CONTACT** WITH MEN FROM OTHER PARTS OF THE STATE AND INTRODUCED HIM TO A NUMBER OF YOUNG **POLITICAL LEADERS.**

LINCOLN WAS STILL A **CANDIDATE** FOR THE ILLINOIS STATE LEGISLATURE. AFTER HIS MILITIA SERVICE ENDED, HE RETURNED TO CAMPAIGNING.

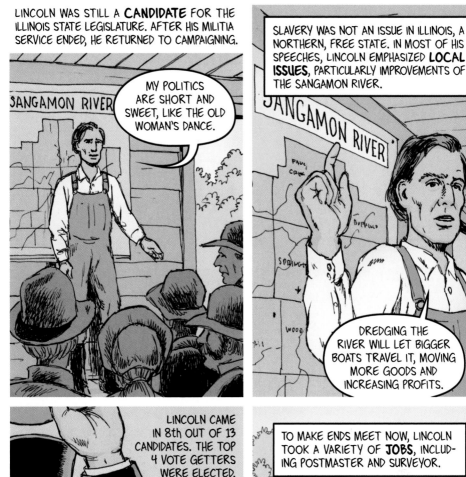

MY POLITICS ARE SHORT AND SWEET, LIKE THE OLD WOMAN'S DANCE.

SLAVERY WAS NOT AN ISSUE IN ILLINOIS, A NORTHERN, FREE STATE. IN MOST OF HIS SPEECHES, LINCOLN EMPHASIZED **LOCAL ISSUES**, PARTICULARLY IMPROVEMENTS OF THE SANGAMON RIVER.

DREDGING THE RIVER WILL LET BIGGER BOATS TRAVEL IT, MOVING MORE GOODS AND INCREASING PROFITS.

LINCOLN CAME IN 8th OUT OF 13 CANDIDATES. THE TOP 4 VOTE GETTERS WERE ELECTED.

I WON!

THOUGH **DISAPPOINTED**, LINCOLN WAS NOT COMPLETELY DISCOURAGED. OF THE 300 VOTES THAT HAD BEEN CAST IN HIS HOMETOWN OF NEW SALEM, HE HAD RECEIVED 277.

TO MAKE ENDS MEET NOW, LINCOLN TOOK A VARIETY OF **JOBS**, INCLUDING POSTMASTER AND SURVEYOR.

TWO YEARS LATER, IN **1834**, LINCOLN RAN AGAIN FOR THE STATE LEGISLATURE.

THIS TIME HE **WON**.

CONGRATULATIONS, ABRAHAM!

THANK YOU, ALL.

NOW THAT LINCOLN WAS GOING TO BE PART OF A **GROUP** TASKED WITH THE MAKING OF **LAWS**, HE DECIDED THAT IT WOULD BE GOOD TO **KNOW** SOMETHING ABOUT THE **SUBJECT**.

LINCOLN BORROWED **LAW BOOKS**. AND AT AN **AUCTION** HE PURCHASED A COPY OF WILLIAM BLACKSTONE'S **COMMENTARIES ON THE LAWS OF ENGLAND**. PUBLISHED IN THE 1760S, IT WAS THE **PRIMARY REFERENCE** FOR THE AMERICAN LEGAL SYSTEM.

HERE YOU ARE.

LINCOLN READ IT **TWICE**, OFTEN COPYING DOWN **ENTIRE PAGES** OF TEXT AND MEMORIZING THEM. HE GOT HIS LAWYER'S LICENSE IN 1836.

AND BECAUSE HE NOW HAD TO ALSO **LOOK** THE PART OF A **LEGISLATOR**, HE BORROWED MONEY FROM A WEALTHY FRIEND SO HE COULD BUY HIS FIRST **SUIT** OF CLOTHES.

YOU'RE LOOKIN' MIGHTY SMART THERE, **MR.** LINCOLN!

LINCOLN SERVED IN THE **ILLINOIS STATE LEG-ISLATURE** FROM 1834 TO 1841 AS A MEMBER OF THE **WHIG PARTY.** THE PARTY'S GOALS WERE TO PROMOTE ECONOMIC GROWTH AND PROTECT AMERICAN COMPANIES FROM BEING TAKEN OVER BY FOREIGN BUSINESSES.

SOUTHERN STATES PASSED LAWS **AGAINST** ABO-LITION SOCIETIES AND DEMANDED THE NORTH DO THE SAME. ILLINOIS, A FREE NORTHERN STATE, HAD A LARGE SOUTHERN-BORN POPULATION. IN 1837, ITS LEGISLATURE PASSED A RESOLUTION **CONDEMNING ABOLITIONIST SOCIETIES.**

FOR MOST OF HIS LIFE, LINCOLN HAD BEEN CON-VINCED SLAVERY WAS WRONG. NOW HE HAD TO MAKE HIS FEELINGS PUBLIC.

DURING THIS PERIOD, THE **ABOLITIONIST MOVEMENT** IN THE NORTH, LED BY **WILLIAM LLOYD GARRISON** AND OTHERS, WAS GAINING STEAM.

SLAVERY IS CRIMINAL AND FULL OF DANGER ... **IT MUST BE BROKEN UP!** WE SHALL ORGANIZE ANTI-SLAVERY SOCIETIES, IF POSSIBLE, IN EVERY CITY, TOWN, AND VILLAGE OF OUR LAND.

MY VOTE ON THE RESOLUTION IS **NAY.**

LINCOLN WAS ONE OF ONLY SIX DISSENTING VOTES. IT WAS HIS FIRST RECORDED **ACTION AGAINST SLAVERY.**

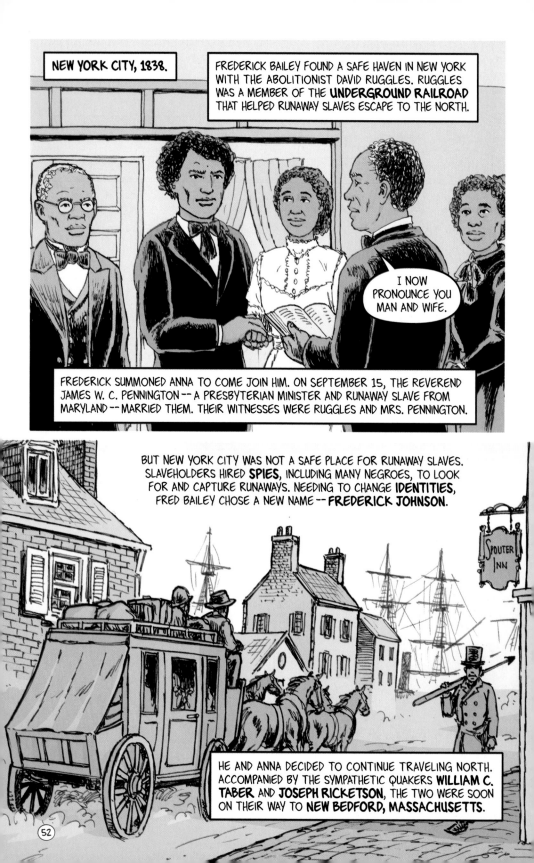

NEW YORK CITY, 1838.

FREDERICK BAILEY FOUND A SAFE HAVEN IN NEW YORK WITH THE ABOLITIONIST DAVID RUGGLES. RUGGLES WAS A MEMBER OF THE **UNDERGROUND RAILROAD** THAT HELPED RUNAWAY SLAVES ESCAPE TO THE NORTH.

I NOW PRONOUNCE YOU MAN AND WIFE.

FREDERICK SUMMONED ANNA TO COME JOIN HIM. ON SEPTEMBER 15, THE REVEREND JAMES W. C. PENNINGTON -- A PRESBYTERIAN MINISTER AND RUNAWAY SLAVE FROM MARYLAND -- MARRIED THEM. THEIR WITNESSES WERE RUGGLES AND MRS. PENNINGTON.

BUT NEW YORK CITY WAS NOT A SAFE PLACE FOR RUNAWAY SLAVES. SLAVEHOLDERS HIRED **SPIES**, INCLUDING MANY NEGROES, TO LOOK FOR AND CAPTURE RUNAWAYS. NEEDING TO CHANGE **IDENTITIES**, FRED BAILEY CHOSE A NEW NAME -- **FREDERICK JOHNSON**.

SPOUTER INN

HE AND ANNA DECIDED TO CONTINUE TRAVELING NORTH. ACCOMPANIED BY THE SYMPATHETIC QUAKERS **WILLIAM C. TABER** AND **JOSEPH RICKETSON**, THE TWO WERE SOON ON THEIR WAY TO **NEW BEDFORD, MASSACHUSETTS**.

IN THE SOUTH, FRED HAD BEEN TAUGHT THAT SLAVERY WAS THE **FOUNDATION** OF ALL **WEALTH** AND SOCIAL STANDING. AND SO THE SIGHTS OF NEW BEDFORD CAME AS A GREAT SURPRISE.

> I ASSUMED EVERYONE HERE WOULD BE POOR. BUT, NATHAN, I FIND HERE AMONG **ALL** CLASSES MORE **WEALTH** THAN I THOUGHT POSSIBLE!

> EVEN HERE, WHERE **LABORERS** LIVE, HOUSES ARE MORE **ELEGANT** AND HAVE MORE **COMFORTS** THAN MANY SLAVEHOLDER HOUSES IN **TALBOT COUNTY.**

> AND **NOT JUST HERE**, FREDERICK, BUT **THROUGHOUT** THE NORTH.

> FREDERICK, I WOULD LIKE TO **DISCUSS** WITH YOU A CHANGE IN **NAME.** THE SURNAME "JOHNSON" IS A COMMON ONE. IN MY EXPERIENCE, THIS HAS CAUSED SOME **CONFUSION.**

> WITH YOUR **PERMISSION**, I WOULD LIKE TO SELECT A NEW NAME FOR YOU.

> VERY WELL. BUT YOU MUST **NOT** TAKE FROM ME THE NAME "FREDERICK." THAT IS MY **IDENTITY.**

> OF COURSE.

> I HAVE JUST FINISHED SIR WALTER SCOTT'S POEM *THE LADY OF THE LAKE.* I WAS IMPRESSED BY ITS HERO, DOUGLAS OF SCOTLAND. I WOULD LIKE TO SUGGEST **"DOUGLAS."**

FREDERICK **AGREED**, ADDING A SECOND "S" BECAUSE HE WAS FAMILIAR WITH **DOUGLASS STREET** IN BALTIMORE. HE WAS NOW, AND WOULD REMAIN FOREVERMORE, **FREDERICK DOUGLASS.**

THESE BARRELS ARE **HEAVY**. AND THE PAY IS **LOW**.

BUT THE WORK IS **STEADY**, FREDERICK.

THREE DAYS AFTER ARRIVING AT NEW BEDFORD, **FREDERICK DOUGLASS** GOT HIS FIRST JOB -- AS A DAY LABORER LOADING BARRELS OF WHALE OIL ONTO SHIPS. THOUGH IT WAS HARD WORK, ALL THE MONEY HE EARNED WAS HIS.

BUT THAT JOY WAS TEMPERED WHEN HE TRIED TO GET A BETTER-PAYING JOB AS A SHIP'S **CAULKER**, SOMETHING HE WAS SKILLED AT. THOUGH THE QUAKER **SHIPOWNER** WAS WILLING...

...THE WHITE SHIP CAULKERS WERE **NOT**. THEY THREATENED TO STRIKE IF DOUGLASS PICKED UP A CAULKING IRON. HE WAS FREE TO WORK AS A LABORER, BUT NOT AS THEIR **EQUAL**.

I'M SORRY, FREDERICK. THE ANSWER IS **NO**.

FOR THE NEXT **THREE YEARS**, FREDERICK WORKED AS A LABORER IN A VARIETY OF JOBS, SOMETIMES ALL DAY AND WELL INTO THE NIGHT. ONE POSITION NO ONE OB-JECTED TO WAS WORKING THE **OVERNIGHT SHIFT** AT A BRASS FOUNDRY.

HIS TASK WAS TO OPER-ATE A **BELLOWS**. AS HE DID SO, HE WOULD READ A CURRENT **NEWSPAPER** HE HAD NAILED TO THE WALL.

SOMEDAY, I WON'T HAVE TO DO THIS. BUT UNTIL THEN...

DOUGLASS SUBSCRIBED TO SEVERAL PAPERS. ONE WAS THE ABOLITIONIST WEEKLY CALLED *THE LIBERATOR*. IT WAS PUBLISHED BY THE **AMERICAN ANTI-SLAVERY SOCIETY** AND EDITED BY WILLIAM LLOYD GARRISON.

IT WAS THE MOST **POPULAR** AS WELL AS THE MOST **HATED** PROTEST PUBLICATION IN THE COUNTRY. GARRISON CHALLENGED CONVENTION IN BOTH THE NORTH AND THE SOUTH BY ADVOCATING **IMMEDIATE EMANCIPATION** AND **EQUALITY** FOR SLAVES.

LYNCH THAT YANKEE!

GARRISON

THE GEORGIA LEGISLATURE OFFERED A **BOUNTY** OF $5,000 (ALMOST **$150,000** IN TODAY'S MONEY) FOR GARRISON'S ARREST AND **DELIVERY** TO THE STATE.

DOUGLASS LATER WROTE OF *THE LIBERATOR*, "THE PAPER BECAME MY MEAT AND MY DRINK."

IT ALSO INSPIRED FREDERICK TO ATTEND **ABOLITION-IST** MEETINGS, EVEN THOUGH HE HAD LITTLE TIME TO SPARE BETWEEN HIS DAY AND HIS NIGHT JOBS.

ABOLITIONISTS, **UNITED** IN THEIR DESIRE TO END SLAVERY, WERE **DIVIDED** IN HOW TO ACCOMPLISH IT.

WELCOME, FREDERICK.

THANK YOU.

ABOLITIONISTS FAVORING **EMANCIPATION** WANTED TO FREE **ALL SLAVES** OVER A SHORT PERIOD OF TIME.

SOME ALSO FAVORED **COLONIZATION**, WHICH WOULD PROVIDE FOR ALL NEGROES TO BE SENT TO AFRICA.

THE COUNTRY OF **LIBERIA** HAS AGREED TO ACCEPT SOME OF OUR SLAVES.

IN 1822, THE **AMERICAN COLONIZATION SOCIETY** FOUNDED THE FIRST SUCH COLONY IN THE WEST AFRICAN NATION OF **LIBERIA**. OTHER COLONIES SOON FOLLOWED.

DOUGLASS **HATED** COLONIZATION. HE HONED HIS SPEAKING SKILLS WITH LEC-TURES **ATTACKING COLONIZATION**.

WE ARE **AMERICAN CITIZENS**, BORN WITH NATURAL, INHER-ENT, JUST, AND INALIENABLE RIGHTS.

MR. GARRISON, I AM A GREAT ADMIRER OF YOURS.

IT IS A PLEASURE TO MEET YOU, MR. DOUGLASS.

ON AUGUST 9, 1841, DOUGLASS **MET** WILLIAM LLOYD GARRISON AT AN ABO-LITIONIST MEETING IN NEW BEDFORD. THE TWO BECAME INSTANT **FRIENDS**.

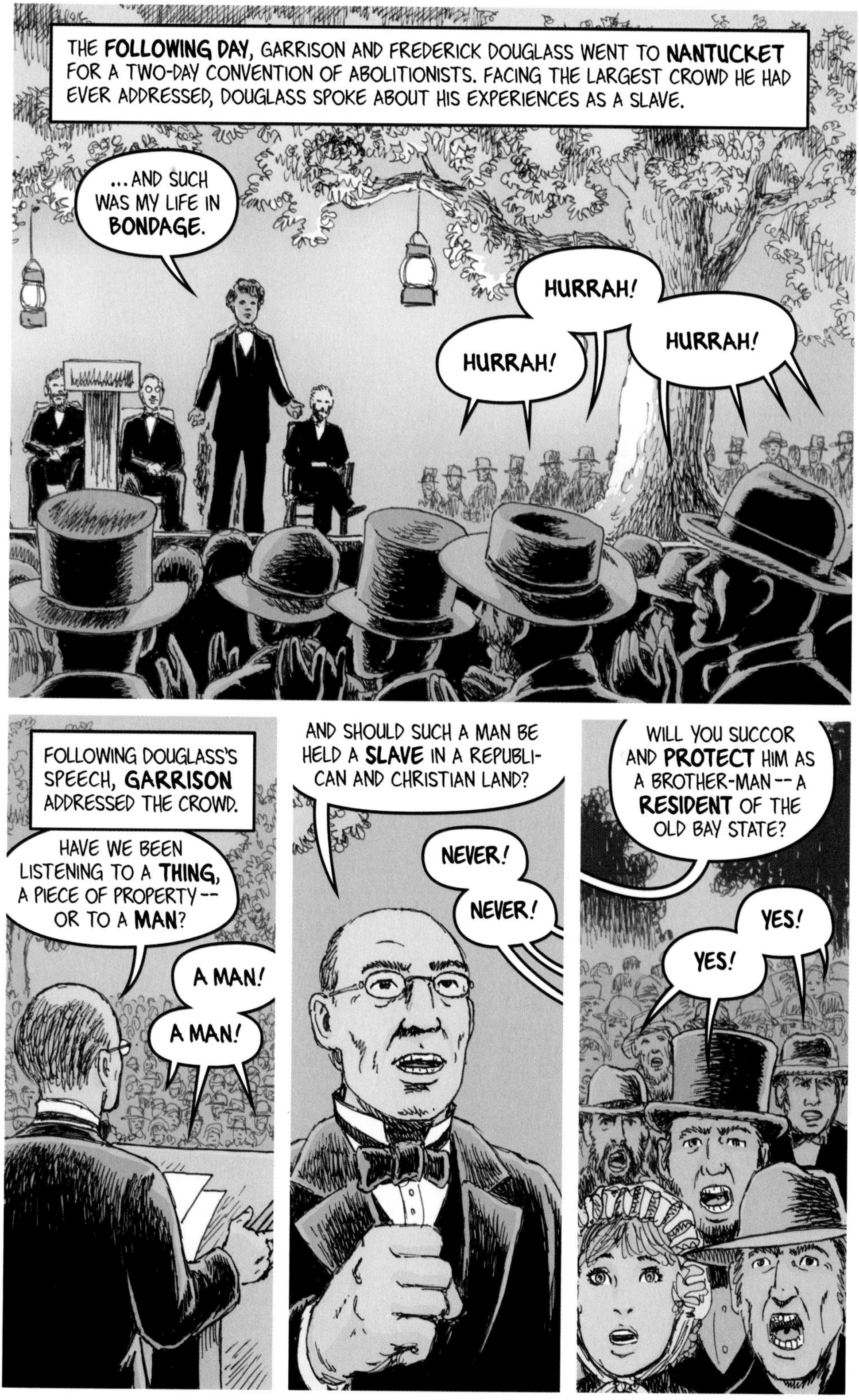
THE **FOLLOWING DAY**, GARRISON AND FREDERICK DOUGLASS WENT TO **NANTUCKET** FOR A TWO-DAY CONVENTION OF ABOLITIONISTS. FACING THE LARGEST CROWD HE HAD EVER ADDRESSED, DOUGLASS SPOKE ABOUT HIS EXPERIENCES AS A SLAVE.
...AND SUCH WAS MY LIFE IN **BONDAGE**.
HURRAH!
HURRAH!
HURRAH!
FOLLOWING DOUGLASS'S SPEECH, **GARRISON** ADDRESSED THE CROWD.
HAVE WE BEEN LISTENING TO A **THING**, A PIECE OF PROPERTY-- OR TO A **MAN**?
A MAN!
A MAN!
AND SHOULD SUCH A MAN BE HELD A **SLAVE** IN A REPUBLICAN AND CHRISTIAN LAND?
NEVER!
NEVER!
WILL YOU SUCCOR AND **PROTECT** HIM AS A BROTHER-MAN-- A **RESIDENT** OF THE OLD BAY STATE?
YES!
YES!

AT THE END OF THE CONVENTION, FREDERICK DOUGLASS WAS APPROACHED BY A **LECTURE CIRCUIT PROMOTER** AND AGREED TO A CONTRACT THAT WOULD PAY HIM $450 A YEAR -- ALMOST **$15,000** IN TODAY'S MONEY.

THIS WILL GREATLY HELP THE CAUSE OF ABOLITION!

DOUGLASS'S ARRIVAL HELPED THE ANTI-SLAVERY SOCIETY. THOUGH THE MOVEMENT HAD GROWN, THE SOCIETY HAD SHRUNK. MEMBERS **JEALOUS** OF GARRISON HAD LEFT TO FORM **THEIR OWN** ORGANIZATIONS. ONE MAJOR RIVAL WAS THE **LIBERTY PARTY**.

LIBERTY PARTY

ABOLITION NOW!

SOUTHERN ORGANIZATIONS PRODUCED PUBLICATIONS FOR DISTRIBUTION IN THE NORTH DESIGNED TO **COUNTER** THE ABOLITIONISTS. BOOKS AND PAMPHLETS BY GEORGE FITZHUGH, SAMUEL CARTWRIGHT, AND OTHERS SHOWED SLAVERY IN AN **IDYLLIC LIGHT**.

CANNIBALS ALL! OR SLAVES WITHOUT MASTERS
George Fitzhugh

SOME, LIKE THE REVEREND THORNTON STRING-FELLOW, USED **THE BIBLE** TO **JUSTIFY SLAVERY**.

HERE, IN EXODUS, CHAPTER 21, VERSES 2, 3, AND 4, AND ELSEWHERE IN THE BIBLE, IS THE **AUTHORITY**, FROM GOD HIMSELF, TO HOLD MEN AND WOMEN, AND THEIR CHILDREN, IN **SLAVERY** AND TO TRANSMIT THEM AS PROPERTY **FOREVER**.

ANOTHER PRO-SLAVERY ADVOCATE WAS E. N. ELLIOTT, THE **PRESIDENT** OF **PLANTERS' COLLEGE** IN MISSISSIPPI.

ABOLITIONISTS ARE FLOODING THE WHOLE COUNTRY WITH THE MOST FALSE AND MALICIOUS **MISREPRESENTATIONS** OF SOCIETY IN SLAVE STATES.

...LEFT UNCHALLENGED, THEY WILL INSPIRE...A CIVIL WAR -- WITH ALL ITS **HORRIBLE** CONSEQUENCES.

THE MASSACHUSETTS ANTI-SLAVERY SOCIETY INVITED FREDERICK DOUGLASS TO SPEAK.

DOUGLASS WAS THE **FIRST** SLAVE WILLING TO STAND BEFORE NORTHERN AUDIENCES **EAGER TO HEAR FROM A SLAVE** WHAT THE INSTITUTION WAS REALLY LIKE.

MANY **SKEPTICS** REFUSED TO BELIEVE DOUGLASS HAD EVER BEEN A SLAVE. IN RESPONSE, **JOHN COLLINS**, A VETERAN LECTURER OF THE MASSACHUSETTS SOCIETY, SAID...

YES, MY BLOOD HAS SPRUNG OUT AS THE LASH EMBEDDED ITSELF IN MY FLESH.

MR. DOUGLASS IS A **GRADUATE OF SLAVERY**...WITH THE DIPLOMA **WRITTEN ON HIS BACK!**

THE AUDIENCE WAS **HORRIFIED**. THIS WAS THEIR FIRST LOOK AT THE **BRU-TALITY** OF **SLAVERY** IN THE FLESH.

THE LECTURE CIRCUIT WAS THE MOST POPULAR **ENTERTAINMENT** OF THE DAY. A SKILLED LECTURER COULD QUICKLY BECOME **FAMOUS**. WITHIN A YEAR, FREDERICK DOUGLASS'S **REPUTATION** WAS MADE.

AUDIENCES EVERYWHERE WERE **SPELLBOUND**.

IN 1843, DOUGLASS WAS PART OF A GROUP OF LECTURERS ORGANIZED TO RALLY THE NORTH TO THEIR CAUSE. IT BEGAN IN NEW HAMPSHIRE AND WORKED ITS WAY WEST.

IN PENDLETON, INDIANA, **RACIST THUGS** MOBBED THE STAGE.

HE'S JUST AN UPPITY **RUNAWAY SLAVE!** KILL HIM!

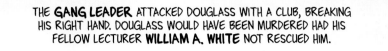

THE **GANG LEADER** ATTACKED DOUGLASS WITH A CLUB, BREAKING HIS RIGHT HAND. DOUGLASS WOULD HAVE BEEN MURDERED HAD HIS FELLOW LECTURER **WILLIAM A. WHITE** NOT RESCUED HIM.

VERY FEW ABOLITIONISTS BELIEVED IN **RACIAL EQUALITY** AS DOUGLASS DID. HE MADE MANY OF THEM UNCOMFORTABLE. EVEN HIS REFINED MANNER OF SPEAKING WAS **CRITICIZED**.

PEOPLE WON'T BELIEVE YOU EVER WAS A SLAVE, FREDERICK, IF YOU KEEP ON THIS WAY.

BETTER HAVE A LITTLE OF THE **PLANTATION MANNER** OF SPEECH THAN NOT...

...'TIS NOT BEST THAT YOU SEEM TOO **LEARNED**.

THOUGH THE **COMMENTS** ABOUT HIS SPEAKING ABILITY AND KNOWLEDGE WERE **INSULTING**, THEY WERE NOT ENTIRELY OFF THE MARK. DOUGLASS *HAD* WORKED HARD TO SCRUB THE "PLANTATION MANNER" FROM HIS SPEECH. AND HE HAD WORKED EVEN HARDER TO **EDUCATE** HIMSELF.

DOUBTS ABOUT HIS CLAIMS OF LIVING A SLAVE'S LIFE **GREW**. IN 1844, ONE **JOURNALIST** WROTE OF A DOUGLASS LECTURE, "MANY PERSONS IN THE AUDIENCE ... COULD NOT BELIEVE THAT HE WAS ACTUALLY A SLAVE. HOW A MAN, ONLY SIX YEARS OUT OF BONDAGE, AND WHO HAD NEVER GONE TO SCHOOL A DAY IN HIS LIFE, COULD SPEAK WITH SUCH **ELOQUENCE** -- WITH SUCH **PRECISION OF LANGUAGE** AND **POWER OF THOUGHT** -- THEY WERE UTTERLY AT A **LOSS** TO DEVISE."

NO SLAVE *I* KNOW SOUNDS LIKE HIM.

YOU THINK HE'S **LYING**?

DOUGLASS DECIDED TO **SILENCE** THOSE CRITICS ONCE AND FOR ALL. HE WOULD **WRITE HIS LIFE'S STORY** IN UNCENSORED DETAIL AND HAVE IT PUBLISHED.

"I WAS BORN IN TUCKAHOE, NEAR HILLSBOROUGH, AND ABOUT TWELVE MILES FROM EASTON, IN TALBOT COUNTY, MARYLAND."

"I HAVE NO ACCURATE KNOWLEDGE OF MY AGE ..."

THIS IS **TERRIBLE!**

NARRATIVE OF THE LIFE OF FREDERICK DOUGLASS

HIS AUTOBIOGRAPHY WAS TITLED *NARRATIVE OF THE LIFE OF FREDERICK DOUGLASS*. IT WAS PUBLISHED BY THE AMERICAN ANTI-SLAVERY SOCIETY IN **MAY 1845**. IT BECAME A **CRITICALLY ACCLAIMED INTERNATIONAL BESTSELLER**.

THREE MONTHS LATER, FREDERICK DOUGLASS HAD TO FLEE AMERICA FOR HIS LIFE.

DOUGLASS RECOUNTED **ABUSES** IN UNVARNISHED DETAIL. THOMAS AULD WAS **FURIOUS** ABOUT HOW HE AND HIS BROTHER, HUGH, WERE DEPICTED.

HE'S A **LIAR**!

BUT HUGH'S RESPONSE WAS MORE OMINOUS AND **DIRECT**, BECAUSE HE ACTUALLY **STILL OWNED** FREDERICK.

I WILL SPARE NO EXPENSE IN ORDER TO **REGAIN POSSESSION** OF HIM!

AND ONCE I HAVE HIM...

...I'LL **SEND HIM TO THE COTTON FIELDS** OF THE SOUTH.

THREE YEARS EARLIER, IN 1842, THE **SUPREME COURT** HAD RULED THAT FREE STATES **DID NOT HAVE THE AUTHORITY** TO PROTECT RUNAWAY SLAVES FROM RETURN TO THEIR MASTERS.

BECAUSE HE WAS NOW SO **FAMOUS**, IT WOULD BE EASY FOR ANYONE TO FIND DOUGLASS AND, WITH A BIT OF HELP, **KIDNAP** AND **RETURN** HIM TO HUGH AULD FOR THE BOUNTY ON HIS HEAD.

I MUST LEAVE.

QUICKLY!

TO **PREVENT** THAT FROM HAP-PENING, AND WITH THE HELP OF FRIENDS, DOUGLASS **LEFT** FOR A LECTURE TOUR OF **GREAT BRITAIN** IN AUGUST 1845.

NOVEMBER 4, 1842, WAS A JOYOUS DAY FOR ABRAHAM LINCOLN. AFTER A THREE-YEAR COURTSHIP, **MARY TODD** WAS TO BECOME HIS **WIFE**. THE CEREMONY WAS HELD IN THE MANSION OF MARY'S SISTER ELIZABETH AND HER HUSBAND, NINIAN EDWARDS.

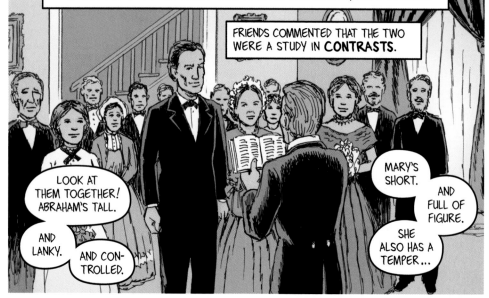

FRIENDS COMMENTED THAT THE TWO WERE A STUDY IN **CONTRASTS**.

LOOK AT THEM TOGETHER! ABRAHAM'S TALL.

AND LANKY.

AND CON-TROLLED.

MARY'S SHORT.

AND FULL OF FIGURE.

SHE ALSO HAS A TEMPER...

UNLIKE LINCOLN, WHO GREW UP POOR, MARY WAS THE DAUGHTER OF A RICH KENTUCKY SLAVEHOLDER.

SHE'S MARRYING **BENEATH** HER STATION. AND THEY'RE GOING TO LIVE IN **ILLINOIS**, SO SHE'LL HAVE TO KEEP UP HER HOME **WITHOUT** SLAVE HELP.

BUT HUSBAND AND WIFE WERE BOTH INTELLIGENT AND POLIT-ICALLY **AMBITIOUS**. THOUGH THE TRANSITION TO MARRIED LIFE **WITHOUT SLAVES OR SERVANTS** WAS DIFFICULT FOR HER AT FIRST, MARY ADAPTED.

APPROXIMATELY NINE MONTHS AFTER THE WEDDING, **ROBERT TODD LINCOLN** WAS BORN. THREE YEARS LATER, THE LINCOLNS WOULD HAVE A SECOND SON, EDWARD.

LINCOLN HAD LEFT POLITICS IN 1841 AND ESTABLISHED A SUCCESSFUL **LAW PRACTICE** WITH HIS PARTNER, WILLIAM H. HERNDON. BUT IN 1846 HE DECIDED TO RUN FOR **CONGRESS** ON THE WHIG TICKET -- HIS FIRST ATTEMPT AT NATIONAL OFFICE --

WE'RE OFF TO WASHINGTON, MARY!

-- AND **WON.**

ON DECEMBER 2, 1847, HE ARRIVED IN WASHINGTON, D.C., THE NEWEST CONGRESSMAN FROM THE STATE OF ILLINOIS.

WASHINGTON WAS THE LARGEST CITY THE LINCOLNS HAD EVER SEEN. IT WAS A TEEMING METROPOLIS OF **40,000 PEOPLE** -- INCLUDING 2,000 SLAVES AND 8,000 FREE NEGROES.

THOUGH IT WAS ONE OF THE **LARGER CITIES** IN THE COUNTRY, MANY OF ITS BACKYARDS MORE RESEMBLED COUNTRY **BARNYARDS** THAN URBAN AREAS.

WASHINGTON, D.C., ALSO HAD ONE OF THE NATION'S **LARGEST SLAVE MARKETS.** IT STOOD JUST A FEW BLOCKS AWAY FROM THE **CAPITOL BUILDING.**

LINCOLN WAS SHOCKED AND DISGUSTED. SOON ENOUGH, HE WOULD HAVE OPPORTUNITIES TO ACT **AGAINST SLAVERY** BOTH IN D.C. AND ON A NATIONAL LEVEL.

SO CLOSE TO THE CAPITOL. IT'S A DISGRACE.

SLAVE SALES

THOUGH LINCOLN WAS NEW TO THE **FEDERAL** LEGISLATURE, HIS FOUR TERMS IN **STATE OFFICE** SERVED HIM WELL IN HIS NEW DUTIES.

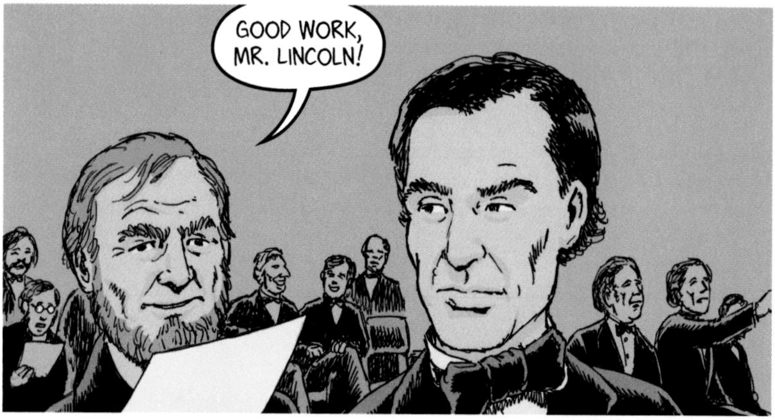
GOOD WORK, MR. LINCOLN!

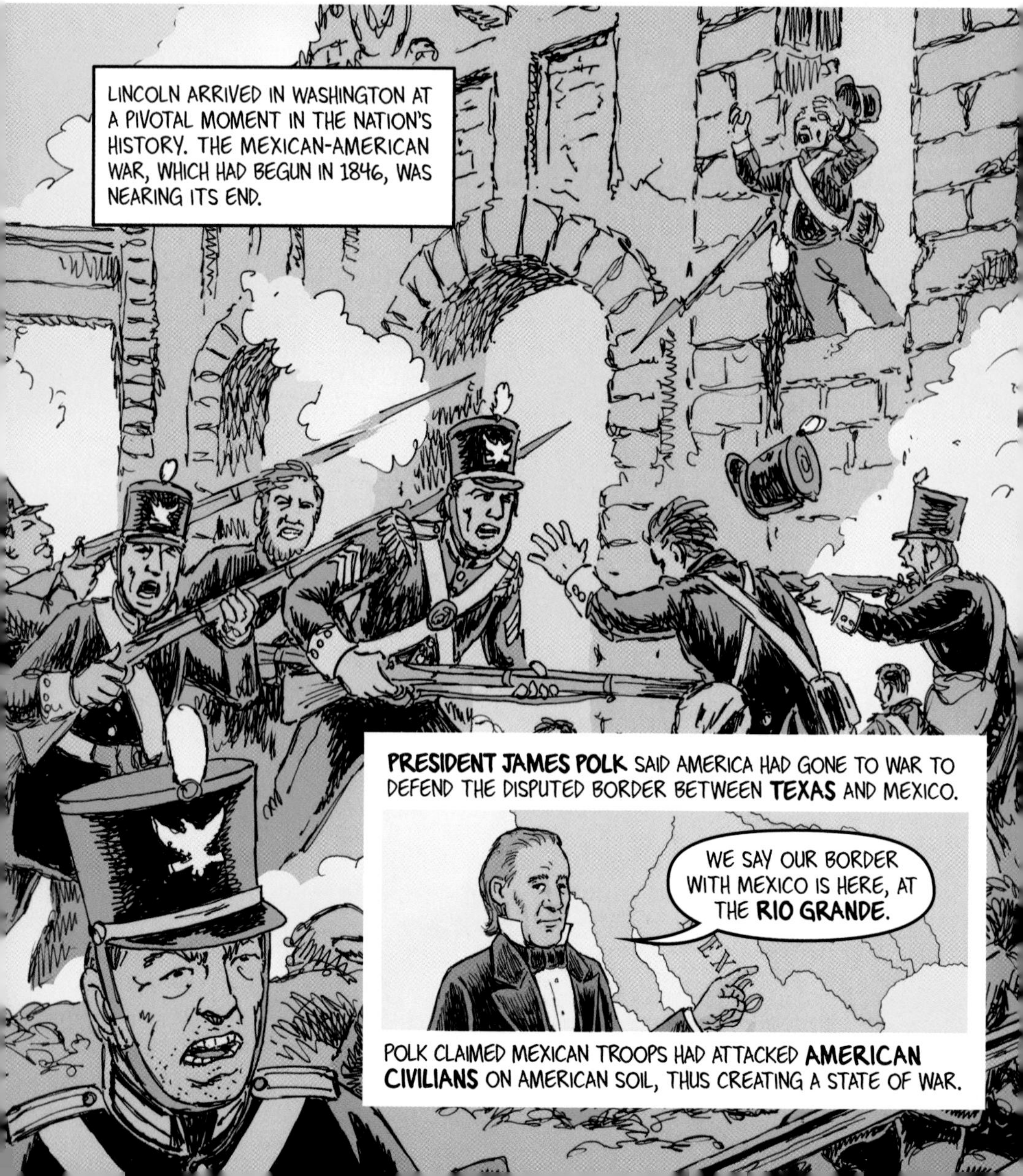
LINCOLN ARRIVED IN WASHINGTON AT A PIVOTAL MOMENT IN THE NATION'S HISTORY. THE MEXICAN-AMERICAN WAR, WHICH HAD BEGUN IN 1846, WAS NEARING ITS END.
PRESIDENT JAMES POLK SAID AMERICA HAD GONE TO WAR TO DEFEND THE DISPUTED BORDER BETWEEN **TEXAS** AND MEXICO.
WE SAY OUR BORDER WITH MEXICO IS HERE, AT THE **RIO GRANDE**.
POLK CLAIMED MEXICAN TROOPS HAD ATTACKED **AMERICAN CIVILIANS** ON AMERICAN SOIL, THUS CREATING A STATE OF WAR.

BUT LINCOLN AND HIS FELLOW WHIGS SAW THE WAR FOR WHAT IT REALLY WAS -- AN OUT-AND-OUT **LANDGRAB** OF ALMOST THE ENTIRE **NORTHERN HALF** OF MEXICO.

THE PRESIDENT WANTS ALL OF MEXICO FROM TEXAS TO CALIFORNIA --

-- AND HE'S LOOKING AT **MORE!**

ON DECEMBER 22, 1847, THE NEWLY ELECTED CONGRESSMAN ABRAHAM LINCOLN TOOK A PUBLIC STANCE AGAINST THE WAR. HE ISSUED SIX OFFICIAL **RESOLUTIONS** CHALLENGING THE PRESIDENT'S REASONS FOR GOING TO WAR.

WE ARE DESIROUS TO OBTAIN A FULL KNOWLEDGE OF ALL THE FACTS...

...WHICH GO TO ESTABLISH WHETHER THE PARTICULAR **SPOT** ON WHICH THE **BLOOD** OF OUR CITIZENS WAS SO **SHED** WAS OR WAS NOT AT THAT TIME **OUR OWN SOIL.**

BUT MOST AMERICANS, PARTICULARLY IN ILLINOIS, **HAD FAVORED** THE MEXICAN WAR AND THE POTENTIAL **INCREASE** OF TERRITORY. PRESIDENT POLK IGNORED LINCOLN, WHO BECAME AN OBJECT OF **SCORN** AMONG HIS FELLOW LEGISLATORS.

THERE GOES "SPOTTY" LINCOLN!

HIS RESOLUTIONS NEVER CAME TO A VOTE.

WITH THE NATION ABOUT TO ACQUIRE SUBSTANTIAL **LAND** FROM MEXICO AS A RESULT OF THE WAR, THE QUESTION AROSE WHETHER THE NEW TERRITORY SHOULD BE FREE OR SHOULD ALLOW SLAVERY.

HERE WAS LINCOLN'S **OPPORTUNITY**. WHILE ACKNOWLEDGING THAT THE CONSTITUTION ALLOWED SLAVERY TO CONTINUE WHERE IT ALREADY EXISTED, LINCOLN SPOKE AGAINST SLAVERY'S **EXTENSION**.

WE SHOULD **NEVER**...FIND NEW PLACES FOR **SLAVERY** TO LIVE IN.

HE SPONSORED **RESOLUTIONS** FOR THE DISTRICT OF COLUMBIA THAT RECOMMENDED THE **GRADUAL ABOLITION OF SLAVERY** AND **COMPENSATED EMANCIPATION**. THEY DID NOT PASS.

ZACHARY TAYLOR WON THE PRESIDENTIAL ELECTION IN 1848. LINCOLN HAD SUPPORTED HIM AND HOPED TO GET A JOB IN THE NEW ADMINISTRATION, BUT HE DID NOT.

ON **MARCH 3, 1849**, LINCOLN'S TERM AS CONGRESSMAN FROM ILLINOIS **ENDED**.

AS HE HAD SAID HE WOULD SERVE ONLY **ONE TERM**, LINCOLN AND HIS FAMILY RETURNED TO **SPRINGFIELD**, WHERE HE RESUMED HIS LAW PRACTICE. ONCE AGAIN, IT SEEMED THAT HIS **POLITICAL CAREER** WAS **OVER**.

FREDERICK DOUGLASS HAD **LEFT** THE UNITED STATES ON AUGUST 16, 1845. AFTER LECTURING FOR FOUR MONTHS IN IRELAND, HE ARRIVED IN **SCOTLAND** IN JANUARY 1846.

WELCOME TO **EDINBURGH**, MR. DOUGLASS!

FOR THE NEXT **15 MONTHS** HE WOULD TRAVEL THROUGHOUT SCOTLAND AND ENGLAND, DELIVERING LECTURES.

DOUGLASS SOON FOUND HIMSELF **CAPTIVATED** BY ENGLAND AND ITS PEOPLE AND MADE NUMEROUS FRIENDS.

WHEN YOUR GOVERNMENT FINALLY ENDED SLAVERY IN ITS TERRITORY ON AUGUST 1, 1834, BY EMANCIPATING 800,000 SLAVES IN THE WEST INDIES, IT WAS THE GREATEST AND GRANDEST EVENT OF THE CENTURY.

LET US HOPE YOUR COUNTRY WILL END SLAVERY SOON AS WELL, MR. DOUGLASS.

I WOULD LIKE TO PROPOSE A TOAST. TO THE ELOQUENT **LION OF ABOLITION**... MR. FREDERICK DOUGLASS...

MR. FREDERICK DOUGLASS!

WHEN HIS ENGLISH FRIENDS HEARD OF HUGH AULD'S **THREAT** TO RE-ENSLAVE DOUGLASS, THEY **PURCHASED** FREDERICK'S **FREEDOM** -- RAISING ABOUT $700 AND SENDING IT TO HUGH AULD.

ON **APRIL 20, 1847,** FREDERICK DOUGLASS RETURNED TO LYNN, MASSACHUSETTS... A **FREE MAN.** HIS WIFE, DAUGHTER, ROSETTA, AND SONS, LEWIS, FRED JUNIOR, AND CHARLES, WERE OVERJOYED.

WELCOME HOME, FREDERICK!

NOW THAT HE WAS BACK, DOUGLASS PREPARED HIMSELF TO FINALLY MAKE THE NEXT **BIG MOVE** IN HIS LIFE. HE WAS GOING TO **LEAVE** THE ANTI-SLAVERY SOCIETY AND START HIS OWN **NEWSPAPER.**

IT'S TIME I DO **MORE!**

DOUGLASS HAD CONCEIVED THIS IDEA AS EARLY AS 1842. AT ONE POINT, HE VOICED HIS DESIRE TO WILLIAM GARRISON AND OTHER ANTI-SLAVERY SOCIETY LEADERS. THEY TRIED TO CONVINCE HIM TO **ABANDON** THAT PLAN.

FREDERICK, YOUR TALENTS ARE THOSE OF A **SPEAKER,** NOT AN EDITOR.

INSTEAD, I PRO-POSE YOU WRITE A COLUMN FOR OUR OFFICIAL PUBLICATION, THE **NATIONAL ANTI-SLAVERY STANDARD.**

DOUGLASS STAYED WITH THE SOCIETY, BUT THE FIRE TO CREATE HIS OWN PUBLIC VOICE BURNED INSIDE.

THIS IS A BRAVE THING YOU'RE DOING, FREDERICK!

FINALLY, HE DISCUSSED HIS **PLANS** FOR A NEWSPAPER WITH THE FRIENDS HE'D MADE IN ENGLAND AND IRELAND. THEY EAGERLY **DONATED** THE **MONEY** TO GET HIM STARTED.

IT WAS A **DIFFICULT DECISION**. DOUGLASS'S MENTOR, WILLIAM LLOYD GARRISON, HAD TREATED HIM LIKE A **FAVORITE SON**. BUT GARRISON WAS ALSO DOMINEERING -- AND INTOLERANT OF ANY OPINIONS THAT DID NOT MATCH HIS OWN.

I AM SORRY MY DECISION WILL WRECK MY FRIENDSHIP.

BUT THIS IS SOMETHING I MUST DO!

KNOWING THE **UGLY SCENE** THAT WOULD ERUPT IF HE TOLD GARRISON FACE-TO-FACE, DOUGLASS DECIDED TO KEEP HIS PLAN A **SECRET**.

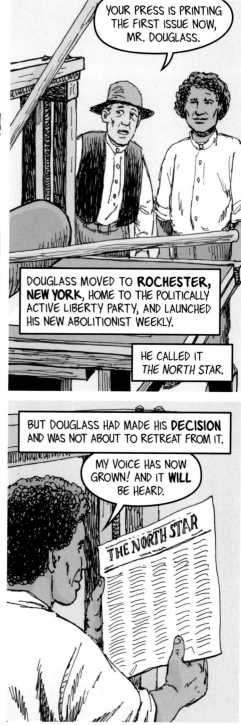

YOUR PRESS IS PRINTING THE FIRST ISSUE NOW, MR. DOUGLASS.

DOUGLASS MOVED TO **ROCHESTER, NEW YORK**, HOME TO THE POLITICALLY ACTIVE LIBERTY PARTY, AND LAUNCHED HIS NEW ABOLITIONIST WEEKLY.

HE CALLED IT *THE NORTH STAR*.

AS DOUGLASS HAD ANTICIPATED, WHEN GARRISON FOUND OUT, HE WAS **FURIOUS** AND NEVER FORGAVE DOUGLASS. OTHER MEMBERS OF THE SOCIETY WERE ALSO **OUTRAGED**.

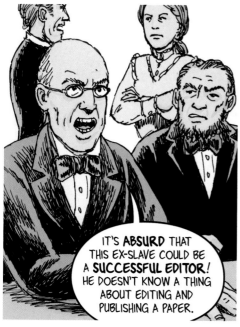

IT'S **ABSURD** THAT THIS EX-SLAVE COULD BE A **SUCCESSFUL EDITOR!** HE DOESN'T KNOW A THING ABOUT EDITING AND PUBLISHING A PAPER.

BUT DOUGLASS HAD MADE HIS **DECISION** AND WAS NOT ABOUT TO RETREAT FROM IT.

MY VOICE HAS NOW GROWN! AND IT **WILL** BE HEARD.

THE NORTH STAR

HE WOULD USE HIS NEWSPAPER AS **HIS PLATFORM** TO EXPOSE, DENOUNCE, PROD, HARASS...AND **DEMAND** AN END TO SLAVERY AND RACISM IN AMERICA.

IN THE PAGES OF DOUGLASS'S *NORTH STAR*, NO **STATESMAN** WAS ABOVE ATTACK. A FAVORITE TARGET WAS **HENRY CLAY, THE SENATOR** FROM KENTUCKY -- A SLAVE STATE.

CLAY WAS KNOWN AS **"THE GREAT COMPROMISER"** BECAUSE OF HIS LEGISLATIVE SKILL ON CONTROVERSIAL ISSUES, PARTICULARLY SLAVERY.

BUT DOUGLASS ATTACKED CLAY AS A **HYPOCRITE**, AND WORSE. DOUGLASS REPEATEDLY CHALLENGED HOW CLAY COULD, ON THE ONE HAND, CLAIM TO **HATE SLAVERY** WHILE, ON THE OTHER, CONTINUE TO **OWN** ABOUT 50 **SLAVES**.

DOUGLASS WOULD ALSO PUBLISH LISTS OF HOUSE AND SENATE VOTES ON ISSUES REGARDING SLAVERY. IN **JANUARY 1849**, A HOUSE RESOLUTION TO **PROHIBIT** THE SLAVE TRADE IN THE DISTRICT OF COLUMBIA WAS PUT TO A VOTE.

aniel Gott
aleb. B. Smith
braham Linco
rt Giddir
m Nam

A **FRESHMAN CONGRESSMAN** NAMED ABRAHAM LINCOLN HAD VOTED WITH THE MAJORITY TO **RETAIN** SLAVERY IN D.C., BUT LINCOLN HAD VOTED THAT WAY BECAUSE HE BELIEVED IT WAS UP TO **LOCAL CITIZENS** -- NOT CONGRESS -- TO DECIDE THE ISSUE.

IN ONE RESPECT, THOUGH, GARRISON AND THE OTHERS WERE RIGHT: DOUGLASS **DIDN'T KNOW ANYTHING** ABOUT EDITING AND PUBLISHING A NEWSPAPER.

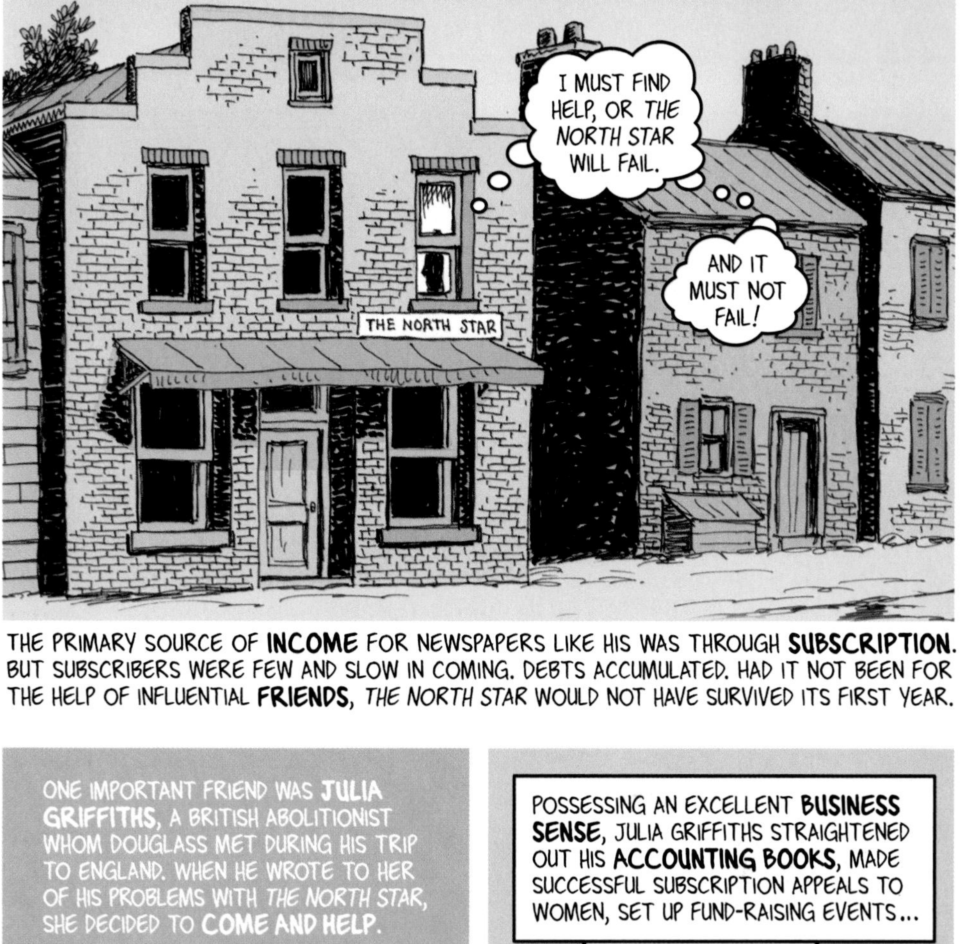
I MUST FIND HELP, OR *THE NORTH STAR* WILL FAIL.
AND IT MUST NOT FAIL!
THE NORTH STAR

THE PRIMARY SOURCE OF **INCOME** FOR NEWSPAPERS LIKE HIS WAS THROUGH **SUBSCRIPTION**. BUT SUBSCRIBERS WERE FEW AND SLOW IN COMING. DEBTS ACCUMULATED. HAD IT NOT BEEN FOR THE HELP OF INFLUENTIAL **FRIENDS**, *THE NORTH STAR* WOULD NOT HAVE SURVIVED ITS FIRST YEAR.

ONE IMPORTANT FRIEND WAS **JULIA GRIFFITHS**, A BRITISH ABOLITIONIST WHOM DOUGLASS MET DURING HIS TRIP TO ENGLAND. WHEN HE WROTE TO HER OF HIS PROBLEMS WITH *THE NORTH STAR*, SHE DECIDED TO **COME AND HELP**.

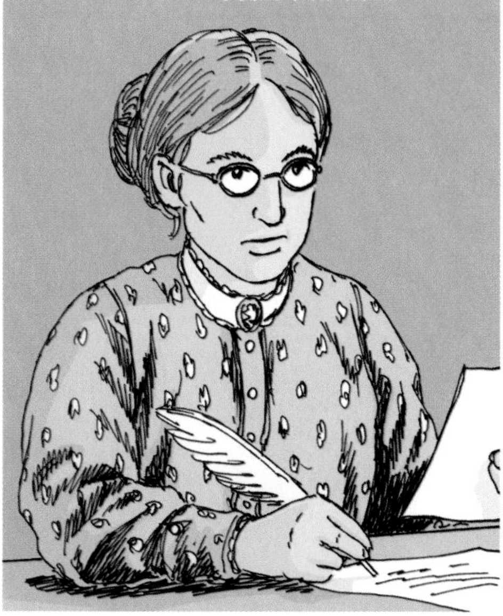

POSSESSING AN EXCELLENT **BUSINESS SENSE**, JULIA GRIFFITHS STRAIGHTENED OUT HIS **ACCOUNTING BOOKS**, MADE SUCCESSFUL SUBSCRIPTION APPEALS TO WOMEN, SET UP FUND-RAISING EVENTS...

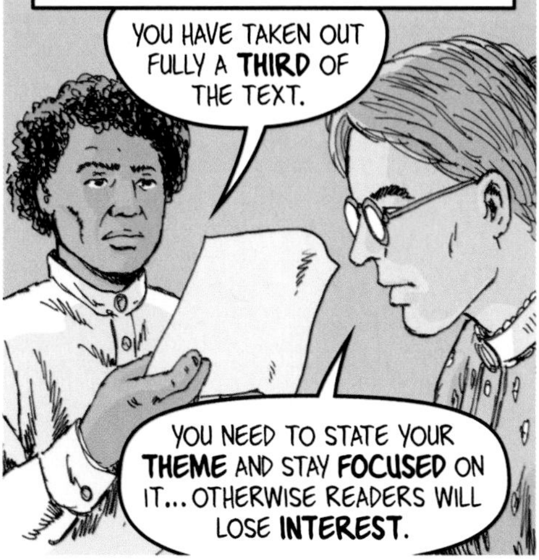
YOU HAVE TAKEN OUT FULLY A **THIRD** OF THE TEXT.
YOU NEED TO STATE YOUR **THEME** AND STAY **FOCUSED** ON IT... OTHERWISE READERS WILL LOSE **INTEREST**.

...AND TAUGHT DOUGLASS HOW TO PROPERLY SPELL AND **EDIT**. HE LEARNED QUICKLY.

DOUGLASS AND GRIFFITHS CAUSED A **STIR** WHEN THEY WALKED DOWN THE STREETS TOGETHER **ARM IN ARM**, AS WAS THE CUSTOM OF THE TIME.

CAN YOU BELIEVE THAT?

IT'S SHOCKING!

AND WHEN IT WAS LEARNED THAT GRIFFITHS WAS STAYING AT DOUGLASS'S **HOME**, RUMORS OF **IMMORALITY** ABOUNDED.

BUT DOUGLASS KNEW THAT IF HE DID **ANYTHING** IMPROPER, WORD WOULD GET OUT AND HIS HARD-FOUGHT **REPUTATION** WOULD BE **RUINED**. NO EVIDENCE OF IMPROPRIETY OF ANY SORT EVER SURFACED.

ANOTHER IMPORTANT **BENEFACTOR** DURING THIS PERIOD WAS THE PHILANTHROPIST AND MEMBER OF THE NATIONAL LIBERTY PARTY **GERRIT SMITH**.

HE USED PART OF HIS WEALTH TO SUPPORT DOUGLASS'S PAPER, AND HE HELPED DOUGLASS HONE HIS POLITICAL VIEWS.

I AM PROUD TO SUPPORT YOU, MR. DOUGLASS.

SMITH AND DOUGLASS DISCUSSED HOW TO **INTERPRET** THE U.S. CONSTITUTION. ON THE ONE HAND, IT STATED THAT "ALL MEN ARE CREATED EQUAL." BUT ON THE OTHER, IT IMPLIED THAT SLAVES SHOULD BE CONSIDERED AS **PROPERTY** RATHER THAN AS PEOPLE.

MR. GARRISON SAYS THE CONSTITUTION IS AN **AGREEMENT** WITH HELL.

THE FACT THAT THE NATION FAVORS AND **UPHOLDS SLAVERY** PROVES **NOTHING** AGAINST THE CONSTITUTION.

FREDERICK, THERE IS NOT ONE PRO-SLAVERY LINE, **NOT ONE LINE** THAT, JUSTLY INTERPRETED, CONTRIBUTES TO THE **UPHOLDING** OF SLAVERY.

IN FACT, I WOULD SAY THE CONSTITUTION PROMOTES THE **ANTI-SLAVERY** CAUSE.

SMITH POINTED OUT THAT THE CONSTI-TUTION NEVER ONCE USES THE **WORD** "SLAVE" OR "SLAVERY," OR "NEGRO." BUT IT DOES MENTION SECURING AND PROTECTING **INDIVIDUAL LIBERTIES**.

THE CONSTITUTION NEEDS TO BE ADMINISTERED ONLY **ACCORDING TO ITS PRINCIPLES.**

DOING SO WILL CAUSE A SPEEDY **OVERTHROW** OF THE WHOLE SYSTEM OF AMERICAN SLAVERY.

HE ARGUED THAT THE CLAUSES USED TO SUPPORT SLAVERY WERE **MISINTERPRETATIONS.** FOR INSTANCE, THE "FUGITIVE" CLAUSE COULD REFER TO APPRENTICES AND CHILDREN THAT HAD RUN AWAY -- **NOT SLAVES.**

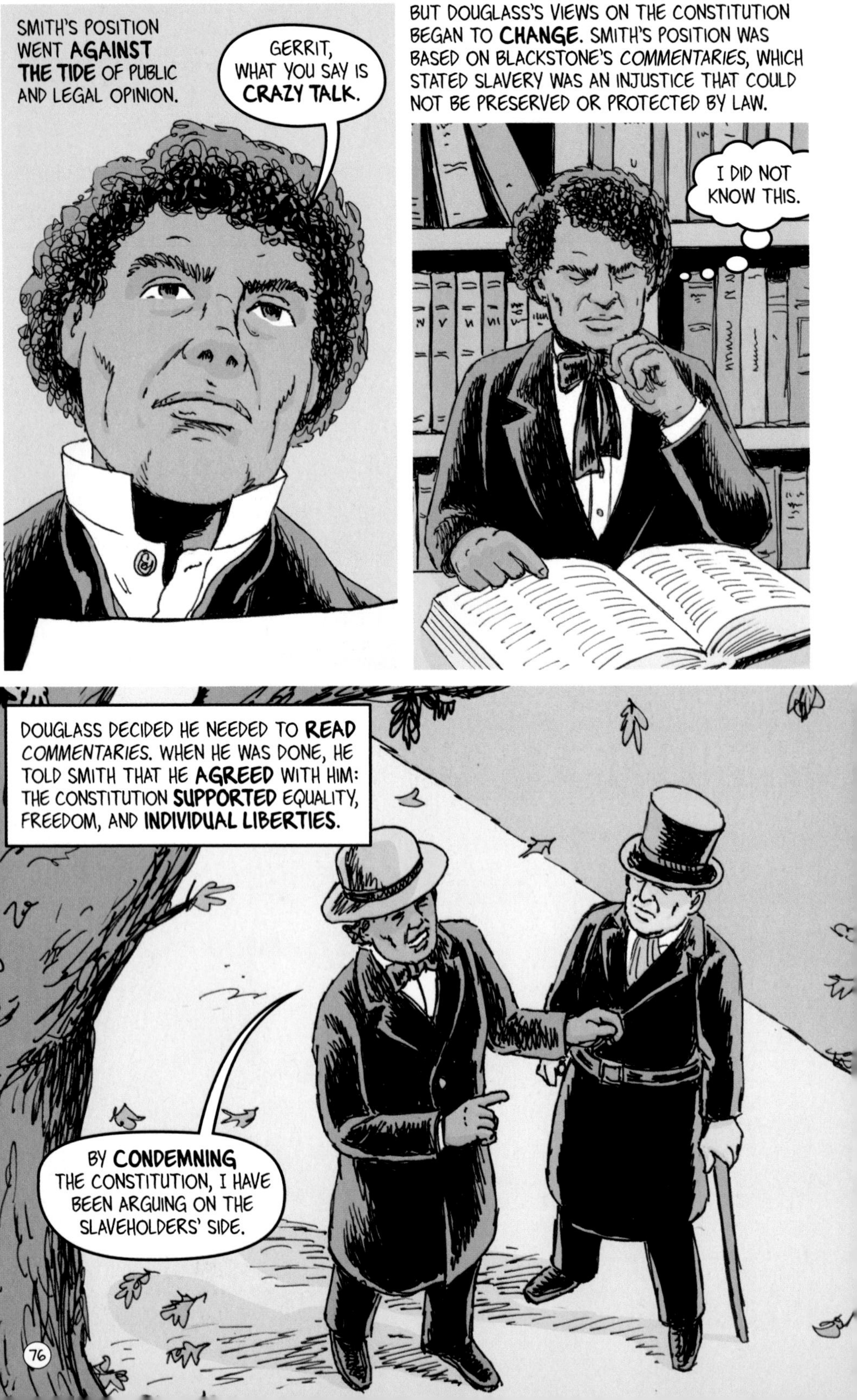
SMITH'S POSITION WENT AGAINST THE TIDE OF PUBLIC AND LEGAL OPINION.
GERRIT, WHAT YOU SAY IS CRAZY TALK.
BUT DOUGLASS'S VIEWS ON THE CONSTITUTION BEGAN TO CHANGE. SMITH'S POSITION WAS BASED ON BLACKSTONE'S COMMENTARIES, WHICH STATED SLAVERY WAS AN INJUSTICE THAT COULD NOT BE PRESERVED OR PROTECTED BY LAW.
I DID NOT KNOW THIS.
DOUGLASS DECIDED HE NEEDED TO READ COMMENTARIES. WHEN HE WAS DONE, HE TOLD SMITH THAT HE AGREED WITH HIM: THE CONSTITUTION SUPPORTED EQUALITY, FREEDOM, AND INDIVIDUAL LIBERTIES.
BY CONDEMNING THE CONSTITUTION, I HAVE BEEN ARGUING ON THE SLAVEHOLDERS' SIDE.

THEN, IN **1850**, WHAT WAS KNOWN AS **THE COMPROMISE** WAS PASSED BY CONGRESS. PUT TOGETHER BY SENATOR HENRY CLAY, IT GAVE SOMETHING TO BOTH PRO-SLAVERS AND ABOLITIONISTS.

THIS IS A GREAT VICTORY FOR OUR NATION!

THE QUESTION OF **SLAVERY** IN THE NEWLY ACQUIRED **NEW MEXICO** AND **UTAH** TERRITORIES **WOULD BE LEFT TO A VOTE** OF THE PEOPLE WHO LIVED THERE. MOST WERE NOT SOUTHERNERS, AND COTTON PLANTATIONS DID NOT FARE WELL IN THE DRY SOUTHWEST. IT WAS A PARTIAL VICTORY FOR ABOLITION.

BUT THE COMPROMISE ALSO HAD A NEW FUGITIVE SLAVE ACT.

IT SAID THAT NO FREE STATE COULD BE A HAVEN FOR RUNAWAY SLAVES. IT **REQUIRED** ORDINARY CITIZENS TO **HELP SLAVE CATCHERS**, AND HELPING A FUGITIVE SLAVE COULD RESULT IN A STEEP FINE AND A PRISON TERM.

THIS IS AN ABOMINATION!

FREDERICK DOUGLASS'S EDITORIAL ATTACKING THE LEGISLATION APPEARED IN *THE NORTH STAR* ON FEBRUARY 8, 1850.

This "compromise" gives everything to liberty in words and secures everything to slavery in deeds... Slavery has no rights!

ABRAHAM LINCOLN, ON THE OTHER HAND, TOOK AN OPTIMISTIC VIEW OF CLAY'S COMPROMISE.

I HAVE **ALWAYS BEEN OPPOSED** TO SLAVERY. I BELIEVE THIS COMPROMISE GIVES THE NATION TIME TO **ELIMINATE SLAVERY** IN A GRADUAL WAY.

IN JUNE 1851, FREDERICK DOUGLASS DECIDED TO JOIN GERRIT SMITH'S NATIONAL LIBERTY PARTY AND USE HIS NEWSPAPER TO HELP PROMOTE IT. HE CHANGED ITS NAME TO *FREDERICK DOUGLASS' PAPER.*

I AM PLEASED TO PRESENT MR. FREDERICK DOUGLASS.

IN 1852, DOUGLASS WAS INVITED BY THE **ROCHESTER LADIES' ANTI-SLAVERY SOCIETY** TO DELIVER A SPEECH ON THE **FOURTH OF JULY.** HE AGREED TO SPEAK -- BUT ON THE **FIFTH** OF JULY.

THE BLESSINGS IN WHICH YOU, THIS DAY, REJOICE ARE NOT ENJOYED IN COMMON. THIS FOURTH OF JULY IS **YOURS**, NOT MINE. **YOU** MAY REJOICE, I MUST **MOURN**.

I SEE THIS DAY FROM THE SLAVE'S POINT OF VIEW... WHAT, TO THE **AMERICAN SLAVE**, IS YOUR FOURTH OF JULY?

A DAY THAT REVEALS TO HIM... **GROSS INJUSTICE** AND **CRUELTY**...

FOR REVOLTING **BARBARITY** AND SHAMELESS **HYPOCRISY**, AMERICA REIGNS WITHOUT A RIVAL.

DOUGLASS DETAILED HOW THE NATION'S **INSTITUTIONS**, INCLUDING THE CHRISTIAN CHURCH, HAD **FAILED TO ELIMINATE** SLAVERY. THEN, AS HIS SPEECH NEARED ITS END, HE ADDRESSED THE **CONSTITUTION**.

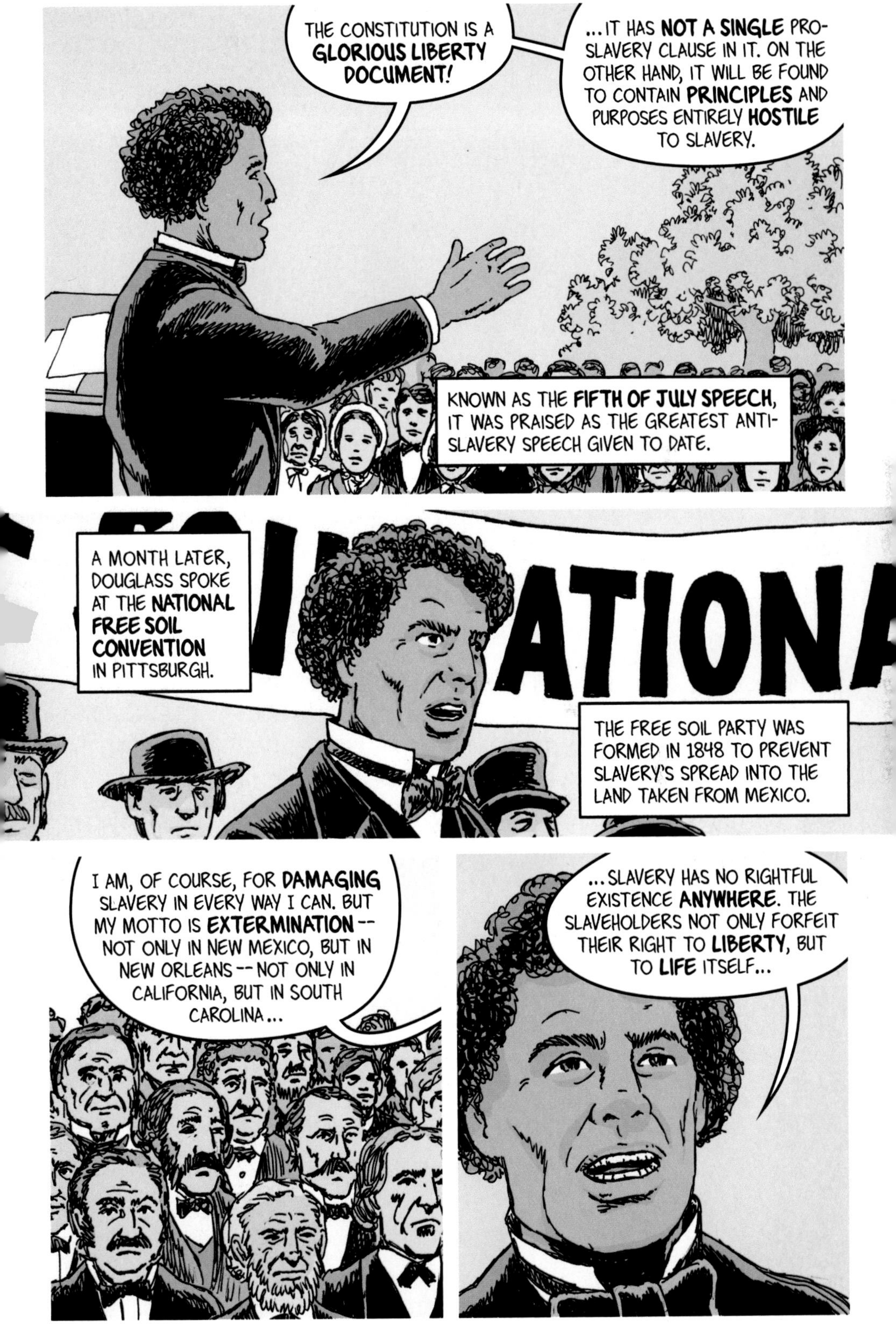
THE CONSTITUTION IS A GLORIOUS LIBERTY DOCUMENT!
...IT HAS NOT A SINGLE PRO-SLAVERY CLAUSE IN IT. ON THE OTHER HAND, IT WILL BE FOUND TO CONTAIN PRINCIPLES AND PURPOSES ENTIRELY HOSTILE TO SLAVERY.
KNOWN AS THE FIFTH OF JULY SPEECH, IT WAS PRAISED AS THE GREATEST ANTI-SLAVERY SPEECH GIVEN TO DATE.
A MONTH LATER, DOUGLASS SPOKE AT THE NATIONAL FREE SOIL CONVENTION IN PITTSBURGH.
ATIONA
THE FREE SOIL PARTY WAS FORMED IN 1848 TO PREVENT SLAVERY'S SPREAD INTO THE LAND TAKEN FROM MEXICO.
I AM, OF COURSE, FOR DAMAGING SLAVERY IN EVERY WAY I CAN. BUT MY MOTTO IS EXTERMINATION-- NOT ONLY IN NEW MEXICO, BUT IN NEW ORLEANS--NOT ONLY IN CALIFORNIA, BUT IN SOUTH CAROLINA...
...SLAVERY HAS NO RIGHTFUL EXISTENCE ANYWHERE. THE SLAVEHOLDERS NOT ONLY FORFEIT THEIR RIGHT TO LIBERTY, BUT TO LIFE ITSELF...

SLAVERY MAKES IT **CRIMINAL** TO CARRY OUT THE **PRINCIPLES** OF **CHRISTIANITY.** IT FORBIDS YOU THE RIGHT **TO DO RIGHT** -- FORBIDS YOU TO SHOW **MERCY** -- FORBIDS YOU TO FOLLOW THE EXAMPLE OF THE **GOOD SAMARITAN.**

I HOPE, THEREFORE, THAT YOU WILL TAKE THE GROUND THAT THIS **SLAVERY** IS A SYSTEM, NOT ONLY OF **WRONG,** BUT OF A **LAWLESS CHARACTER,** AND **CANNOT** BE CHRISTIANIZED NOR LEGALIZED.

IN **11 YEARS,** DOUGLASS HAD GONE FROM BEING A **FUGITIVE RUNAWAY SLAVE** TO BEING THE MOST **FAMOUS ABOLITIONIST** IN THE NATION.

IN THAT RESPECT, HIS LIFE EXEMPLIFIED THE AMERICAN DREAM OF **OPPORTUNITY FOR ALL** AND **SUCCESS THROUGH HARD WORK** -- THOUGH MUCH OF HIS LIFE AND WORK REMAINED BEFORE HIM.

ABRAHAM LINCOLN, TOO, HAD ACHIEVED **HIS OWN VERSION** OF THE AMERICAN DREAM. AFTER HIS BRIEF APPEARANCE IN NATIONAL POLITICS...

...IT SEEMED THE REST OF HIS PROFESSIONAL LIFE WOULD BE THAT OF A SUCCESSFUL **LAWYER** IN HIS HOMETOWN.

THANK YOU, MR. LINCOLN.

THEN, ON MAY 30, 1854, THE **KANSAS-NEBRASKA ACT** BECAME LAW.

EXTRA! PEOPLE IN **TERRITORIES** TO **CHOOSE** WHETHER OR NOT TO **BAN SLAVERY!**

JUST AS IN NEW MEXICO AND UTAH, PEOPLE LIVING IN THOSE TERRITORIES WOULD VOTE ON THE QUESTION OF SLAVERY. BUT UNLIKE THE OTHERS, KANSAS AND NEBRASKA HAD ALREADY BEEN **DESIGNATED** AS **FREE TERRITORIES** BY CONGRESS IN 1820. NOW THEY WERE UP FOR GRABS.

THE ACT HAD BEEN SPONSORED BY SENATOR STEPHEN A. DOUGLAS OF ILLINOIS, A DEMOCRAT.

THIS DOUGLAS SPELLED HIS NAME WITH ONLY ONE "S," AND HE AND LINCOLN KNEW EACH OTHER WELL.

LINCOLN BELIEVED THAT IF SLAVERY COULD BE **PROHIBITED** FROM THE NEW TERRITORIES IN THE WEST, IT WOULD EVENTUALLY **DIE OUT** IN THE SOUTH AS WELL.

I SUPPOSE, **PEACEFULLY,** ITS EXTINCTION WOULD OCCUR IN ABOUT **A HUNDRED YEARS.**

BUT THE KANSAS-NEBRASKA ACT GAVE SLAVERY A NEW **LEASE** ON LIFE. TO TRY TO STOP ITS WESTERN SPREAD, LINCOLN DECIDED TO **REENTER NATIONAL POLITICS.**

81

NO LONGER WAS SLAVERY JUST A NATIONAL ISSUE -- IT WAS THE **MOST IMPORTANT** NATIONAL ISSUE. ALLOWING PEOPLE TO VOTE ON THE ISSUE OF SLAVERY MADE IT **PERSONAL** FOR EVERYONE...AND EVERYONE WAS CONVINCED BLOOD WOULD SOON BE SHED OVER IT.

YOU MUST READ THESE, ABRAHAM.

LINCOLN'S LAW PARTNER, **WILLIAM HERNDON**, WAS AN ARDENT ABOLITIONIST. LINCOLN TOLD HERNDON HE HAD DECIDED TO RUN AGAINST SENATOR DOUGLAS IN THE UPCOMING **ELECTION**. HERNDON BEGAN CLIPPING FOR LINCOLN ARTICLES THAT DISCUSSED SLAVERY.

LINCOLN READ AND STUDIED THEM ALL. WHEN IT CAME TIME FOR HIM TO MOUNT THE STAGE AND PUBLICLY **ARGUE** AGAINST SLAVERY'S SPREAD, HE WOULD BE **READY**.

BY NOW, THE FRAGMENTED WHIG PARTY HAD COLLAPSED, AND MANY ANTI-SLAVERS CHOSE TO JOIN THE RECENTLY FORMED **REPUBLICAN PARTY**. LINCOLN WORKED TO HELP THEM **ORGANIZE** IN ILLINOIS.

WHERE WE FAILED AS **WHIGS**, WE MUST SUCCEED AS **REPUBLICANS**.

IN 1856, LINCOLN SPOKE TO THE DELEGATES IN ILLINOIS WHO WERE CHARGED WITH CREATING THE GOALS AND IDEALS FOR THE NEW PARTY. WHEN THEY ASKED HIS OPINION OF THE KANSAS-NEBRASKA ACT, HE SAID...

UNLESS A CHANGE IS MADE IN OUR PRESENT COURSE, **BLOOD WILL FLOW** ON ACCOUNT OF NEBRASKA, AND **BROTHER'S HAND WILL BE RAISED AGAINST BROTHER!**

THE REPUBLICAN PARTY HELD ITS **FIRST NATIONAL CONVENTION** AND NOMINATED **JOHN C. FRÉMONT** AS ITS CANDIDATE FOR PRESIDENT IN 1856. LINCOLN CAME IN SECOND IN THE NOMINATION FOR VICE PRESIDENT.

James Buchanan

JOHN C. FRÉMONT

THE ELECTION WAS WON BY THE DEMOCRAT **JAMES BUCHANAN.** BUT THE **REPUBLICANS** HAD WON ENOUGH CONGRESSIONAL AND STATE GOVERNMENT SEATS TO BECOME A **RISING FORCE** IN NATIONAL POLITICS.

ON MARCH 6, 1857, THE **SUPREME COURT** HANDED DOWN THE MOST CONTROVERSIAL RULING IN ITS LONG HISTORY, THE **DRED SCOTT** DECISION.

SCOTT, A MISSOURI SLAVE, CLAIMED THAT HE WAS A **FREE MAN** AFTER HIS MASTER TOOK HIM INTO ILLINOIS AND MINNESOTA, STATES THAT **PROHIBITED** SLAVERY.

IN A MAJORITY RULING WRITTEN BY CHIEF JUSTICE ROGER TANEY,* THE COURT STATED THAT AS A NEGRO, SCOTT WAS **NOT** A **CITIZEN**. THEN, IN A PASSAGE THAT BECAME **INFAMOUS**, THE RULING **INTERPRETED THE CONSTITUTION** TO VIEW **ALL NEGROES** AS:

...BEINGS OF AN **INFERIOR ORDER**, AND ALTOGETHER **UNFIT** TO ASSOCIATE WITH THE WHITE RACE, EITHER IN SOCIAL OR POLITICAL RELATIONS, AND **SO FAR INFERIOR** THAT THEY HAD **NO RIGHTS** WHICH THE WHITE MAN WAS BOUND TO RESPECT.

*Pronounced "Tawney."

THE MOST IMPORTANT, CONTROVERSIAL, AND POLITICALLY DIVISIVE FEATURE OF TANEY'S RULING WAS THAT NEITHER CONGRESS NOR A TERRITORIAL LEGISLATURE COULD BAN SLAVERY FROM A TERRITORY. MANY NORTHERNERS WERE SHOCKED BY THE DECISION. SURPRISINGLY, FREDERICK DOUGLASS WAS **PLEASED**. AS HE SAW IT, DRED SCOTT WAS THE **TIPPING POINT**.

SOCIETY

ON MAY 14, 1857, DOUGLASS ANNOUNCED HIS **RESPONSE** IN A SPEECH TO THE AMERICAN ABOLITION SOCIETY IN NEW YORK CITY.

DOUGLASS REPEATEDLY **REMINDED** HIS AUDIENCE THAT WHILE ELECTED OFFICIALS AND JUDGES HAD AUTHORITY, ULTIMATE **POWER** LAY IN **THEIR** HANDS...AND THEY NEEDED TO **EXERCISE** THAT POWER **NOW**.

LINCOLN, TOO, WAS ANGERED BY THE DRED SCOTT DECISION. BUT HIS STYLE WAS TO ATTACK IT WITH **LEGAL ARGUMENT** RATHER THAN MORAL OUTRAGE.

CHIEF JUSTICE TANEY... INSISTS AT GREAT LENGTH THAT **NEGROES WERE NO PART** OF THE PEOPLE WHO MADE, OR FOR WHOM WAS MADE, THE **DECLARATION OF INDEPENDENCE** OR THE **CONSTITUTION** OF THE UNITED STATES.

ON THE CONTRARY, JUDGE CURTIS, IN HIS DISSENTING OPINION, SHOWS THAT IN 5 OF THE THEN 13 STATES, **FREE NEGROES WERE VOTERS...**

...AND THEREFORE **WERE** AMONG THOSE WHO HAD VOTED TO ADOPT THE CONSTITUTION IN THE FIRST PLACE. THEIR VOTES WERE **COUNTED EQUALLY** WITH THOSE OF THE WHITE CITIZENS.

WHILE WHITE ABOLITIONISTS WANTED TO END SLAVERY, FEW OF THEM BELIEVED IN **EQUALITY** OF THE RACES.

BUT LINCOLN MANAGED TO MAKE HIS POINTS WITHOUT OFFENDING MOST VOTERS.

IN THE FOUR YEARS FOLLOWING THE PASSAGE OF THE KANSAS-NEBRASKA ACT, LINCOLN WORKED HARD FOR THE ILLINOIS REPUBLICAN PARTY. AS A REWARD, THE PARTY **NOMINATED** HIM AS THEIR **CANDIDATE** FOR THE UNITED STATES SENATE IN 1858.

HIS OPPONENT WAS THE **INCUMBENT**, SENATOR STEPHEN A. DOUGLAS.

THEIR CONTEST WOULD PRODUCE THE MOST FAMOUS SERIES OF **POLITICAL DEBATES** IN U.S. HISTORY.

IN ACCEPTING HIS PARTY'S NOMINATION, LINCOLN SAID THAT DOUGLAS'S KANSAS-NEBRASKA ACT HAD MADE THINGS **WORSE** FOR EVERYONE.

ABRAHAM LINCOLN FOR SENATOR OF THE REPUBLICAN PAR

IN THE BOOK OF MATTHEW, HE FOUND A WAY TO PHRASE THE CURRENT CONFLICT THAT HIS AUDIENCE WOULD RECOGNIZE:

A HOUSE DIVIDED AGAINST ITSELF CANNOT STAND.

I BELIEVE THIS GOVERNMENT **CANNOT ENDURE** PERMANENTLY **HALF SLAVE** AND **HALF FREE**...

...IT WILL BECOME **ALL** ONE THING, OR ALL THE OTHER.

IN WHAT WOULD LATER BE CALLED HIS **"HOUSE DIVIDED"** SPEECH, LINCOLN RAISED THE ALARM THAT THE ISSUE OF SLAVERY WAS A **NATIONAL CRISIS.**

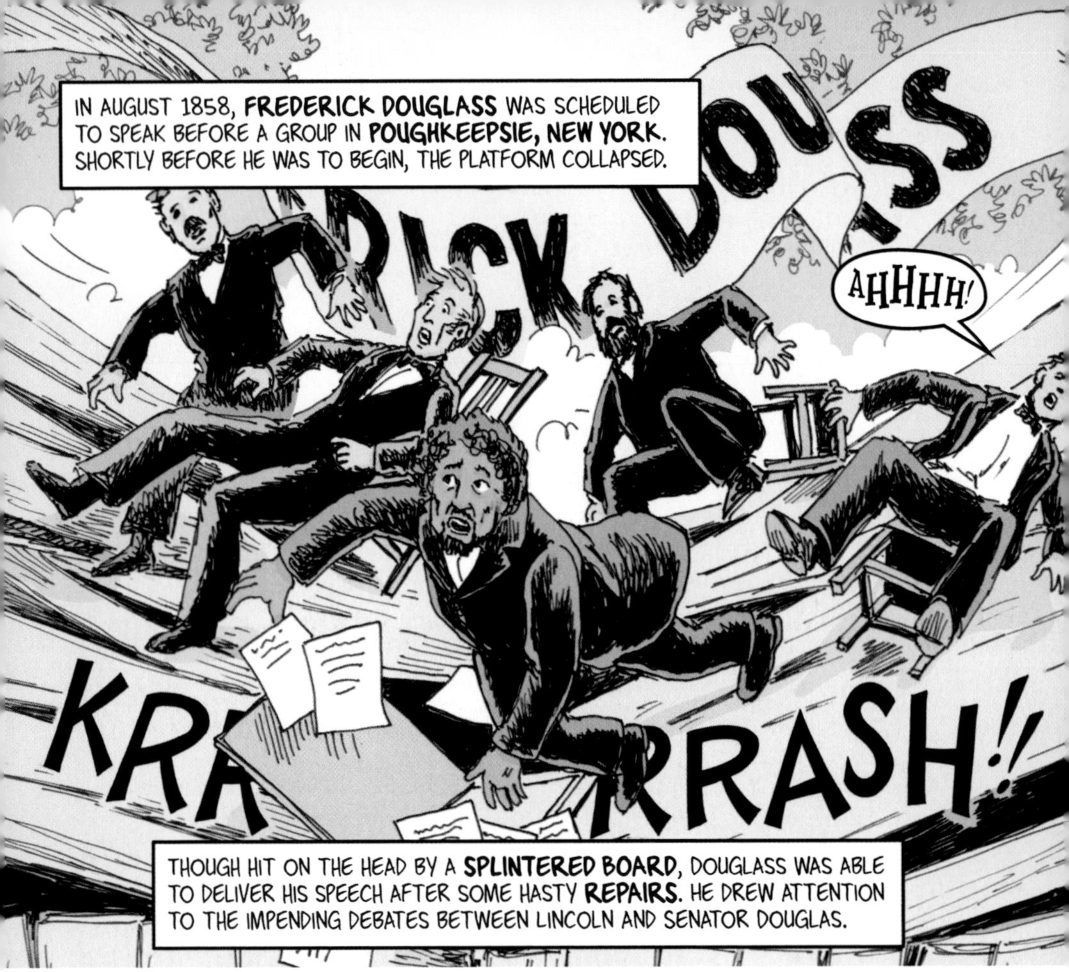
IN AUGUST 1858, **FREDERICK DOUGLASS** WAS SCHEDULED TO SPEAK BEFORE A GROUP IN **POUGHKEEPSIE, NEW YORK**. SHORTLY BEFORE HE WAS TO BEGIN, THE PLATFORM COLLAPSED.
AHHHH!
KRA
RRASH!!
THOUGH HIT ON THE HEAD BY A **SPLINTERED BOARD**, DOUGLASS WAS ABLE TO DELIVER HIS SPEECH AFTER SOME HASTY **REPAIRS**. HE DREW ATTENTION TO THE IMPENDING DEBATES BETWEEN LINCOLN AND SENATOR DOUGLAS.

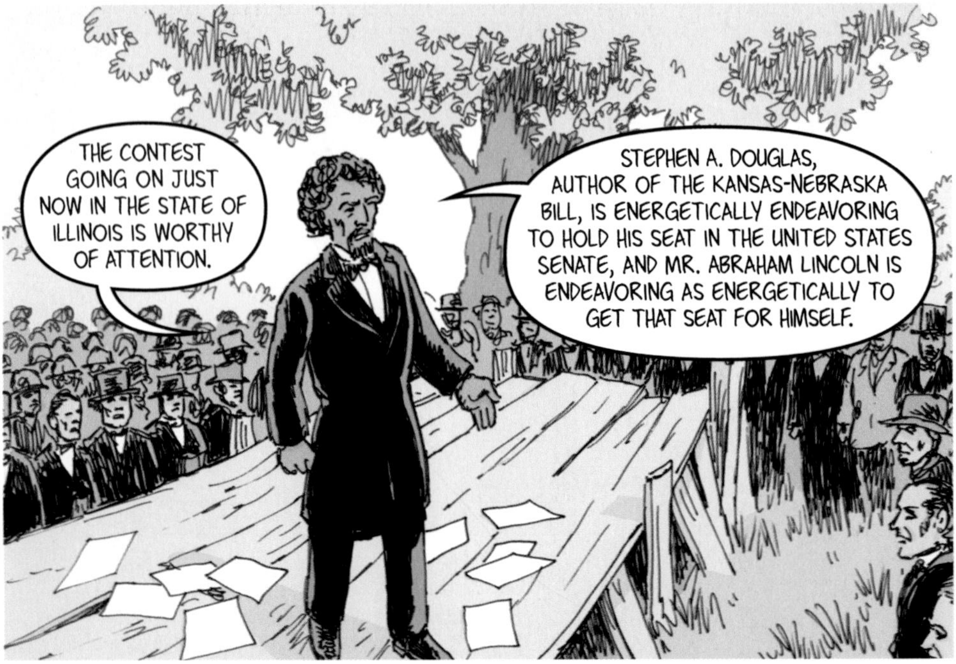
THE CONTEST GOING ON JUST NOW IN THE STATE OF ILLINOIS IS WORTHY OF ATTENTION.
STEPHEN A. DOUGLAS, AUTHOR OF THE KANSAS-NEBRASKA BILL, IS ENERGETICALLY ENDEAVORING TO HOLD HIS SEAT IN THE UNITED STATES SENATE, AND MR. ABRAHAM LINCOLN IS ENDEAVORING AS ENERGETICALLY TO GET THAT SEAT FOR HIMSELF.

THEN DOUGLASS VOICED THE REALITY ON EVERYONE'S MIND.

THE TRUTH IS THAT **SLAVERY** AND **ANTI-SLAVERY** ARE AT THE BOTTOM OF THE CONTEST.

HE POINTED OUT THAT LINCOLN'S ADVERSARY WAS **POPULAR**, HAD MONEY -- AND WAS A DYED-IN-THE-WOOL **RACIST**. HE FURTHER DESCRIBED THE SENATOR AS...

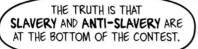

ONE OF THE MOST RESTLESS, AMBITIOUS, BOLDEST, AND MOST **UNSCRUPULOUS ENEMIES** WITH WHOM THE CAUSE OF THE COLORED MAN HAS HAD TO CONTEND.

IT SEEMS TO ME THAT THE **WHITE DOUGLAS** SHOULD OCCASIONALLY MEET HIS JUST DESERTS AT THE HANDS OF A **BLACK ONE**. ONCE I THOUGHT HE WAS ABOUT TO MAKE THE NAME RESPECTABLE, BUT NOW I DESPAIR OF HIM, AND MUST DO THE BEST I CAN FOR IT MYSELF.

I HAVE READ MR. LINCOLN'S "HOUSE DIVIDED" SPEECH WITH **ADMIRATION**. IT IS A GREAT SPEECH.

I NOW LEAVE THE SENATOR IN THE HANDS OF MR. LINCOLN...

AFTER INITIALLY RESISTING, SENATOR DOUGLAS AGREED TO **DEBATE** LINCOLN SEVEN TIMES IN LOCATIONS THROUGHOUT THE STATE OF ILLINOIS.

DOUGLAS, NICKNAMED **THE LITTLE GIANT**, STOOD JUST FIVE FEET FOUR. HE WAS A **DANDY** WHO DRESSED WELL, DRANK HEAVILY, AND SMOKED CIGARS NONSTOP.

LINCOLN DIDN'T DRINK ALCOHOL AND STOOD SIX FEET FOUR, AND HIS **LANKY FRAME** HAD THE RARE ABILITY TO TURN FINE CLOTHES INTO ILL-FITTING GARMENTS.

BUT **BOTH** WERE SMART, **SKILLED DEBATERS**, AND AMBITIOUS. THE **FIRST DEBATE** WAS HELD AT WASHINGTON SQUARE, A PARK IN OTTAWA, ILLINOIS, ON AUGUST 21, 1858.

DOUGLAS TRIED TO PAINT LINCOLN AS A **RADICAL** BENT ON IMPOSING **RACIAL EQUALITY** -- SOMETHING HE KNEW THE NORTHERN WHITE ELECTORATE WOULD NOT ACCEPT.

LINCOLN PARRIED BY REPEATEDLY EMPHASIZING THE **ECONOMIC INJUSTICE** OF SLAVERY.

IN LIGHT OF THE DRED SCOTT DECISION, WHICH PERMITTED SLAVERY EVERYWHERE BY DEFINING NEGROES AS **PROPERTY** AND NOT **PEOPLE**, LINCOLN POSED A SIMPLE QUESTION:

HOW CAN THE PEOPLE OF A TERRITORY **FORBID SLAVERY** FROM THEIR MIDST BEFORE THE TERRITORY BECOMES A STATE?

LINCOLN HAD TRAPPED DOUGLAS. THE SENATOR NEEDED TO MAKE A SIMPLE ANSWER TO A COMPLEX ISSUE.

DOUGLAS PAUSED, CLEARLY UNCOMFORTABLE.

THEN HE SAID...

THEY CAN REFUSE TO ENACT SLAVE CODES TO CONTROL SLAVES, AND THAT WILL DISCOURAGE OWNERS...

THESE WORDS WOULD COME BACK TO HAUNT DOUGLAS WHEN HE SOUGHT THE DEMOCRATIC NOMINATION FOR PRESIDENT IN 1860.

LINCOLN HAD WON THAT EXCHANGE.

BETWEEN DEBATES, EACH CANDIDATE GAVE INDIVIDUAL SPEECHES. ON SEPTEMBER 2, 1858, LINCOLN SPOKE TO A LARGE CROWD IN CLINTON, ILLINOIS.

WHILE MANY WHITE VOTERS SINCERELY WISHED TO END SLAVERY, LINCOLN KNEW THEY DID NOT WANT TO HAVE NEGROES AS NEIGHBORS, DID NOT SEE THEM AS THEIR EQUALS -- AND WOULD NOT ALLOW MIXING OF THE RACES IN MARRIAGE.

BUT SENATOR DOUGLAS WAS **REPEATEDLY SAYING** THAT LINCOLN AND THE REPUBLICANS **WANTED** THESE THINGS. IT WOULD TAKE ALL OF LINCOLN'S SKILL TO BLUNT THOSE CHARGES.

...LET ME SAY A **FEW WORDS** IN REGARD TO DOUGLAS'S GREAT **HOBBY** OF NEGRO EQUALITY.

HE...SAYS...THAT THE REPUBLICAN PARTY IS IN **FAVOR** OF ALLOWING WHITES AND BLACKS TO **INTERMARRY** AND ASSOCIATE ON TERMS OF **PERFECT EQUALITY.**

HE KNOWS THAT WE ADVOCATE **NO** SUCH **DOCTRINES** AS THOSE, BUT HE CARES NOT HOW MUCH HE **MISREPRESENTS** US IF HE CAN GAIN A FEW VOTES BY SO DOING...

SENATOR DOUGLAS IS VERY MUCH AFRAID THAT THE **TRIUMPH** OF THE REPUBLICAN PARTY WILL LEAD TO A GENERAL MIXTURE OF THE WHITE AND BLACK RACES.

PERHAPS I AM WRONG IN SAYING THAT **HE IS AFRAID**...

...SO I WILL CORRECT MYSELF BY SAYING THAT **HE PRETENDS TO FEAR** THAT THE SUCCESS OF OUR PARTY WILL RESULT IN THE AMALGAMATION OF BLACKS AND WHITES. I THINK I CAN SHOW PLAINLY, FROM DOCUMENTS NOW BEFORE ME, THAT DOUGLAS'S FEARS ARE **GROUNDLESS**.

THE **CENSUS OF 1850** TELLS US THAT IN THAT YEAR THERE WERE OVER 400,000 **MULATTOES** IN THE UNITED STATES.

NOW LET US TAKE WHAT IS CALLED AN ABOLITION STATE -- THE REPUBLICAN, SLAVERY-HATING STATE OF NEW HAMPSHIRE -- AND SEE HOW MANY MULATTOES WE CAN FIND WITHIN **HER** BORDERS. THE NUMBER AMOUNTS TO **JUST 184**.

IN THE DEMOCRATIC AND ARISTOCRATIC STATE OF **VIRGINIA**, THERE WERE A **FEW MORE** MULATTOES. HOW MANY DO YOU SUPPOSE THERE WERE? 79,775, WHICH IS **23,000 MORE** THAN THERE WERE **IN ALL THE FREE STATES!**

IN THE **SLAVE STATES** THERE WERE, IN 1850, **348,000** MULATTOES. AND IN THE FREE STATES THERE WERE **LESS THAN 60,000** -- AND A LARGE NUMBER OF THEM WERE IMPORTED FROM THE SOUTH.

SO, IT IS **SLAVERY**, NOT FREEDOM, THAT **CAUSES THE MIXING** OF RACES.

LINCOLN COUNTERED DOUGLAS WITH **FACTS AND NUMBERS**, WHICH MANY FOLKS JUST COULD NOT DENY.

LINCOLN'S **RIGHT**... IF A WHITE MASTER HAS A NEGRO SLAVE WOMAN, HE CAN DO ANYTHING HE WANTS WITH HER... AND SHE **CAN'T** SAY NO.

SOLD!

BUT THE SOUTHERN LEADERSHIP WAS NOT ABOUT TO ADMIT ITS **HYPOCRISY**. FOR THEM, THE SOCIAL AND COMMERCIAL **BENEFITS** OF SLAVERY FAR OUTWEIGHED THE MORAL CONSEQUENCES.

ALTON, ILLINOIS.
OCTOBER 15, 1858.

THE DEBATES CONTINUED IN THE SAME VEIN, WITH EACH SIDE GUILTY OF EXAGGERATING AND MISREPRESENTING THE OTHER'S POSITION. IN ALTON, LINCOLN CHOSE TO USE THIS SEVENTH AND FINAL DEBATE TO SUMMARIZE HIS POSITION.

I LOOK UPON SLAVERY **AS A GREAT EVIL**...

...IT **THREATENS THE EXISTENCE** OF THIS UNION...AND OUR OWN LIBERTY AND PROSPERITY.

AFTER LINCOLN CONCLUDED, SENATOR DOUGLAS ENDED THE DEBATE WITH A RESPONSE THAT FOCUSED ON **HONORING** THE **CONSTITUTION**.

THE ONLY REMEDY AND SAFETY FOR OUR COUNTRY IS THAT WE STAND BY THE CONSTITUTION AS OUR FATHERS MADE IT...OBEY THE LAWS AS THEY ARE PASSED... AND SUSTAIN THE DECISIONS OF THE SUPREME COURT AND THE CONSTITUTED AUTHORITIES.

LINCOLN WON THE POPULAR VOTE. BUT AT THAT TIME, SENATORS WERE SELECTED BY THEIR STATE LEGISLATORS, AND DOUGLAS WAS DECLARED THE WINNER.

IN SEPTEMBER 1859, **FREDERICK DOUGLASS** RECEIVED A LETTER FROM THE MILITANT ABOLITIONIST **JOHN BROWN**, REQUESTING AN URGENT MEETING. DOUGLASS WAS ASKED TO BRING MONEY AND A MUTUAL FRIEND -- SHIELDS GREEN, A RUNAWAY SLAVE.

HELLO, JOHN. WE HAVE BOTH BEEN BUSY SINCE WE LAST MET.

IT IS GOOD TO SEE YOU AGAIN, AFTER SO MANY YEARS, FREDERICK.

DOUGLASS AND BROWN HAD MET IN 1848 AND BECOME FRIENDS. BUT WHILE DOUGLASS **SPOKE ELOQUENTLY** ABOUT ENDING SLAVERY, BROWN TOOK **VIOLENT ACTION**.

HIS SLAUGHTER OF PRO-SLAVERY KANSANS IN 1856 HAD MADE HIM THE MOST **HATED MAN** IN THE SOUTH. NOW BROWN WANTED TO LAUNCH AN **ARMED SLAVE INSURRECTION**.

HIS FIRST TARGET: THE U.S. ARMY ARSENAL AT HARPERS FERRY, VIRGINIA, TO OBTAIN WEAPONS FOR THE SLAVES' REVOLUTION.

COME WITH ME, DOUGLASS. I WILL DEFEND YOU WITH MY LIFE.

IF YOU **ATTACK** HARPERS FERRY, YOU'LL BE ATTACKING THE **FEDERAL GOVERNMENT**, AND THAT WOULD SET THE WHOLE COUNTRY **AGAINST US**.

FINE.

SHIELDS GREEN DECIDED TO THROW HIS LOT IN WITH JOHN BROWN. BUT DOUGLASS HAD A WIFE AND YOUNG FAMILY...

...AND HE WAS CONVINCED BROWN'S PLAN COULD NOT POSSIBLY WORK.

SOMETHING **STARTLING** LIKE THIS IS **JUST** WHAT THE NATION NEEDS.

BROWN AND 21 FOLLOWERS ATTACKED THE ARSENAL ON OCTOBER 16, 1859.

AS DOUGLASS PREDICTED, THE INSURRECTION **FAILED.**

MARINES CAPTURED BROWN AND SEVEN OF HIS FOLLOWERS, KILLING THE REST.

ON DECEMBER 2, JOHN BROWN WAS EXECUTED BY HANGING.

HE HANDED A NOTE TO A GUARD THAT SAID, "I, JOHN BROWN, AM NOW QUITE CERTAIN THAT THE CRIMES OF THIS GUILTY LAND CAN NEVER BE PURGED AWAY BUT WITH BLOOD."

IN BROWN'S POSSESSION WERE DOCUMENTS WITH FREDERICK DOUGLASS'S NAME ON THEM. THE GOVERNOR OF VIRGINIA DEMANDED THAT DOUGLASS BE CAPTURED AND TRIED FOR TREASON.

DOUGLASS KNEW IF THAT HAPPENED, HE'D BE EXECUTED.

HE MANAGED TO ESCAPE ON A SHIP TO CANADA JUST IN TIME.

DOUGLASS CONTINUED ON TO ENGLAND. HIS **EXILE** WAS CUT SHORT WHEN, IN MARCH 1860, HE RECEIVED A **LETTER** INFORMING HIM THAT HIS DAUGHTER ANNIE HAD **DIED**.

BRAVING **ARREST**, HE RETURNED TO ROCHESTER IN APRIL TO BE WITH HIS FAMILY. THOUGH HE RESUMED PUBLISHING HIS **NEWSPAPER**, HE DECIDED NOT TO TRAVEL ON THE LECTURE CIRCUIT UNTIL THINGS HAD CALMED DOWN.

IN **MAY 1860**, AT THE REPUBLICAN NATIONAL CONVENTION IN CHICAGO, IN THE **THIRD ROUND** OF BALLOTING, ABRAHAM LINCOLN WON HIS PARTY'S NOMINATION FOR PRESIDENT OF THE UNITED STATES.

FREDERICK DOUGLASS DECIDED TO THROW HIS FULL SUPPORT, AND THAT OF HIS NEWSPAPER, BEHIND LINCOLN.

MR. LINCOLN IS A MAN OF UNBLEMISHED PRIVATE CHARACTER... HAS A COOL, WELL-BALANCED HEAD; GREAT FIRMNESS OF WILL...

...IS PERSEVERINGLY INDUSTRIOUS; AND ONE OF THE MOST FRANK, HONEST MEN IN POLITICAL LIFE.

WE WOULD PREFER A POLITICAL PARTY THAT CLAIMED "ALL RIGHTS TO ALL MEN." BUT, BECAUSE THAT HAS YET TO HAPPEN,

WHEN LOOKING AT THE CHOICE BETWEEN REPUBLICANS AND DEMOCRATS,

WE CAN BUT DESIRE THE SUCCESS OF THE REPUBLICAN CANDIDATES.

AS THE HISTORIAN JAMES M. McPHERSON NOTED, THE PRESIDENTIAL CAMPAIGN OF 1860 WAS **"UNIQUE"** IN AMERICAN POLITICS.

Abraham Lincoln   Stephen A. Douglas   John Bell   John C. Breckinridge

THE REPUBLICAN PARTY HAD NO PRESENCE IN TEN STATES IN THE SOUTH. THE DEMOCRATIC PARTY HAD **SPLIT** ALONG SECTIONAL LINES, WITH THE NORTH NOMINATING STEPHEN DOUGLAS AND THE SOUTH NOMINATING **JOHN C. BRECKINRIDGE**, WHO WAS JAMES BUCHANAN'S VICE PRESIDENT.

A THIRD PARTY, THE **CONSTITUTIONAL UNION**, ENTERED THE FRAY WITH ITS CANDIDATE, THE FORMER SENATOR **JOHN BELL**, A SLAVEHOLDER FROM TENNESSEE. ESSENTIALLY, **TWO CAMPAIGNS** WERE RUN: LINCOLN VERSUS DOUGLAS IN THE NORTH AND BRECKINRIDGE VERSUS BELL IN THE SOUTH. IN THE END, LINCOLN **WON** WITH 180 ELECTORAL VOTES. DOUGLAS CAME IN A HUMILIATING FOURTH, RECEIVING JUST 12 ELECTORAL VOTES.

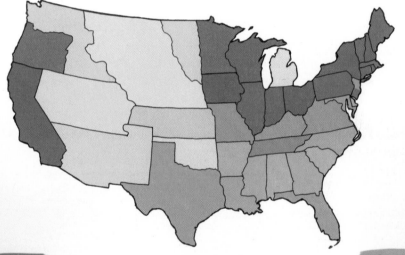

LINCOLN

Maine 8
New Hampshire 5
Vermont 5
Massachusetts 13
Rhode Island 4
Connecticut 6

New York 35
Pennsylvania 27
New Jersey 4
  (split with Douglas)
Ohio 23
Michigan 6

Indiana 13
Illinois 11
Iowa 4
Minnesota 4
California 4 (Lincoln)
Oregon 3 (Lincoln)

DOUGLAS

New Jersey 3
(split with
  Lincoln)
Missouri 9

BRECKINRIDGE

Delaware 3
Maryland 8
Arkansas 4
North Carolina 10

South Carolina 8
Georgia 10
Florida 3
Alabama 9

Mississippi 7
Louisiana 6
Texas 4

BELL

Virginia 15
Kentucky 12
Tennessee 12

MANY SOUTHERNERS HAD THREATENED THAT IF LINCOLN WON, THEY WOULD **SECEDE**. LINCOLN'S VICTORY LED TO CALLS FOR ACTION ACROSS THE SOUTH.

AT HIS HOME IN SPRINGFIELD, LINCOLN **DISMISSED** THOSE STATEMENTS.

IT IS JUST THE **HEAT OF THE MOMENT**. THE SOUTHERN PEOPLE **LOVE** THE UNION TOO MUCH TO LET SECESSION TAKE PLACE.

BUT LINCOLN **MISCALCULATED**. ON DECEMBER 20, 1860, SOUTH CAROLINA **SECEDED FROM THE UNION** AND DECLARED ITSELF THE INDEPENDENT **REPUBLIC OF SOUTH CAROLINA**. WOULD MORE STATES FOLLOW? EVERYTHING DEPENDED ON HOW PRESIDENT-ELECT LINCOLN RESPONDED.

LINCOLN RECEIVED THE **NEWS** LATER THAT DAY WHILE DISCUSSING **CABINET APPOINTMENTS** WITH THE POWERFUL REPUBLICAN POLITICAL BOSS OF NEW YORK, **THURLOW WEED**.

UNLESS YOU WANT A **WAR** ON YOUR HANDS...

...YOU'D BETTER OFFER THE SOUTH A **COMPROMISE** ON SLAVERY IN THE TERRITORIES...THE SOUTH IS TOO WEAK POLITICALLY TO RECOVER THE POWER THEY'VE LOST...WE CAN AFFORD TO BE **GENEROUS**.

BUT LINCOLN WAS UNWILLING TO COMPROMISE IN ALLOWING SLAVERY IN THE WEST.

THE BEST WAY TO AVOID SERIOUS TROUBLE IS THROUGH **WISDOM** AND FORBEARANCE. BUT ON ONE SUBJECT I AM RESOLUTE... THE UNION MUST BE **PRESERVED**.

I HAVE HEARD OF A **COMPROMISE** PROPOSED BY SENATOR JOHN CRITTENDEN OF KENTUCKY CALLING FOR A CONSTITUTIONAL AMENDMENT **GUARANTEEING** SLAVERY IN THE STATES.

I DON'T DESIRE SUCH A **CONSTITUTIONAL AMENDMENT** MYSELF. BUT SINCE THE QUESTION OF SUCH AN AMENDMENT BELONGS TO THE **AMERICAN PEOPLE**, I DON'T FEEL JUSTIFIED...TO WITHHOLD IT FROM THEIR **CONSIDERATION**.

I REMAIN COMMITTED TO THE **RIGHT** OF EACH STATE TO CONTROL ITS OWN **DOMESTIC INSTITUTIONS**.

DESPITE HIS **PERSONAL** HATRED OF SLAVERY, LINCOLN WOULD NOT ALLOW IT TO BE ABOLISHED WHERE IT ALREADY EXISTED, AS HE SAW THIS AS VIOLATING THE CONSTITUTION.

HE WOULD ACT ONLY TO STOP ITS WESTWARD SPREAD, IN THE BELIEF THAT IF IT DID NOT SPREAD, IT WOULD EVENTUALLY DIE OUT.

ON DECEMBER 22, 1860, PRESIDENT-ELECT LINCOLN WROTE TO HIS OLD FRIEND THE FORMER GEORGIA CONGRESSMAN **ALEXANDER H. STEPHENS** WITH WHAT HE HOPED WAS A REASSURANCE THAT WOULD KEEP SLAVE STATES FROM LEAVING THE UNION.

BUT IN THE FOUR MONTHS BETWEEN LINCOLN'S ELECTION AND HIS INAUGURATION, **SEVEN SOUTHERN STATES** SECEDED.

FOLLOWING SOUTH CAROLINA WERE MISSISSIPPI, FLORIDA, ALABAMA, GEORGIA, LOUISIANA, AND TEXAS.

101

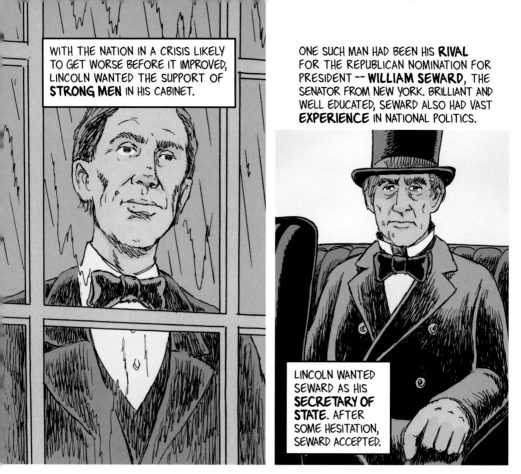

WITH THE NATION IN A CRISIS LIKELY TO GET WORSE BEFORE IT IMPROVED, LINCOLN WANTED THE SUPPORT OF **STRONG MEN** IN HIS CABINET.

ONE SUCH MAN HAD BEEN HIS **RIVAL** FOR THE REPUBLICAN NOMINATION FOR PRESIDENT -- **WILLIAM SEWARD**, THE SENATOR FROM NEW YORK. BRILLIANT AND WELL EDUCATED, SEWARD ALSO HAD VAST **EXPERIENCE** IN NATIONAL POLITICS.

LINCOLN WANTED SEWARD AS HIS **SECRETARY OF STATE**. AFTER SOME HESITATION, SEWARD ACCEPTED.

IN A LETTER TO SEWARD, LINCOLN FOCUSED ON **STOPPING** SLAVERY'S **EXPANSION**.

"ON THE QUESTION OF EXTENDING SLAVERY INTO **NEW TERRITORIES**, I AM **INFLEXIBLE** IN MY OPPOSITION, WITH **ONE** EXCEPTION...IF KEEPING THE UNION TOGETHER MEANS NEW MEXICO MUST ALLOW SLAVERY, THAT IS THE **LIMIT** I WILL GO."

WELL, FATHER, MR. LINCOLN'S CERTAINLY CLEAR IN HIS **ORDERS**. WOULDN'T YOU SAY, MOTHER?

INDEED HE **IS**, FRED.

Chapter Three:
War

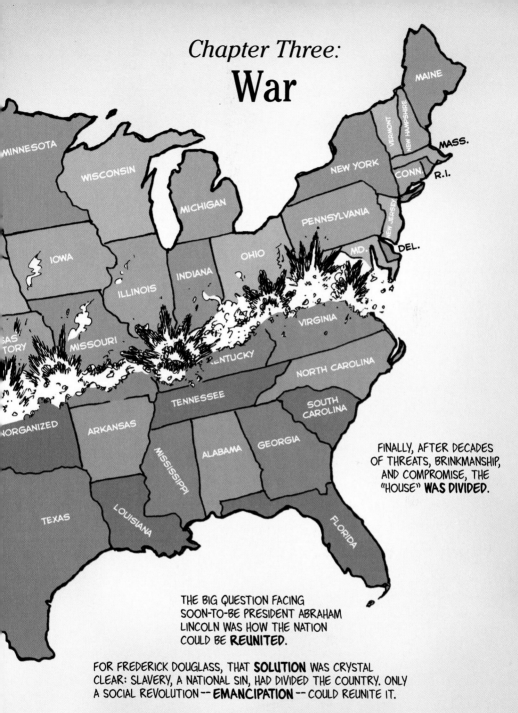

FINALLY, AFTER DECADES OF THREATS, BRINKMANSHIP, AND COMPROMISE, THE "HOUSE" **WAS DIVIDED.**

THE BIG QUESTION FACING SOON-TO-BE PRESIDENT ABRAHAM LINCOLN WAS HOW THE NATION COULD BE **REUNITED.**

FOR FREDERICK DOUGLASS, THAT **SOLUTION** WAS CRYSTAL CLEAR: SLAVERY, A NATIONAL SIN, HAD DIVIDED THE COUNTRY. ONLY A SOCIAL REVOLUTION -- **EMANCIPATION** -- COULD REUNITE IT.

LINCOLN **AGREED** WITH DOUGLASS THAT SLAVERY WAS **EVIL.** BUT LINCOLN WAS PRESIDENT OF THE UNITED STATES AND SWORN TO PRESERVE AND PROTECT THE **CONSTITUTION.** HIS DECISIONS ABOUT UNITING THE NATION AND THE FUTURE OF SLAVERY WOULD DETERMINE THE SUCCESS OR FAILURE OF THIS **SECOND AMERICAN REVOLUTION**...

...BETTER KNOWN TO HISTORY AS THE **AMERICAN CIVIL WAR.**

IN THE WEEKS LEADING UP TO LINCOLN'S INAUGURATION, FREDERICK DOUGLASS PUSHED HARDER THAN EVER FOR **EMANCIPATION**. HE SAW IT CLEARLY AND CORRECTLY AS...

A MATTER OF LIFE AND DEATH, GENTLEMEN!

BUT CONGRESS WAS MOVING IN THE **OPPOSITE DIRECTION** ON THE ISSUE OF SLAVERY. IN AN EFFORT TO ENCOURAGE SECEDED STATES TO **RETURN** TO THE UNION, LOCALITIES ACROSS THE NORTH **RESCINDED ABOLITION LAWS** AND LAWS THAT PROTECTED ESCAPED SLAVES.

THE **MOST IMPORTANT** ATTEMPT WAS MADE IN **CONGRESS**. ON DECEMBER 18, 1860, THE KENTUCKY SENATOR JOHN CRITTENDEN INTRODUCED THE **CRITTENDEN COMPROMISE**. IT SOUGHT TO REVIVE THE 1820 MISSOURI COMPROMISE THAT REGULATED SLAVERY IN THE TERRITORIES.

DISGRACEFULLY, IT ALSO PROPOSED A **CONSTITUTIONAL AMENDMENT** THAT WOULD PLACE THE INSTITUTION OF SLAVERY FOREVER **ABOVE** THE LAW AND **BEYOND** FEDERAL CONTROL.

NEWS OF THE CRITTENDEN COMPROMISE AND LINCOLN'S ACTION REGARDING IT CONFIRMED DOUGLASS'S **FEARS** AND AROUSED HIS FULL **FURY.**

WE ARE NOW IN DANGER OF HAVING A **COVENANT WITH DEATH**... AN AGREEMENT WITH HELL.

DOUGLASS PREDICTED THAT IF THE NORTH **GAVE UP ON** ITS ANTI-SLAVERY STANCE...

THE PLANTATION RULE WILL EXTEND IT-SELF OVER THE NORTH, AND THE NEGRO WILL BE **HATED, PERSECUTED,** AND **DESPISED** AS NEVER BEFORE.

WORSE WAS TO COME. THE OHIO **REPRESENTATIVE THOMAS CORWIN** FOLLOWED UP WITH A FORMAL PROPOSAL: THE CORWIN -- OR THIRTEENTH -- AMENDMENT, TO MAKE SLAVERY A **PERMANENT** PART OF THE CONSTITUTION. ON MARCH 2, 1861, CONGRESS **PASSED** THE AMENDMENT.

THE **NEXT STEP** WAS UP TO THE PRESIDENT-ELECT.

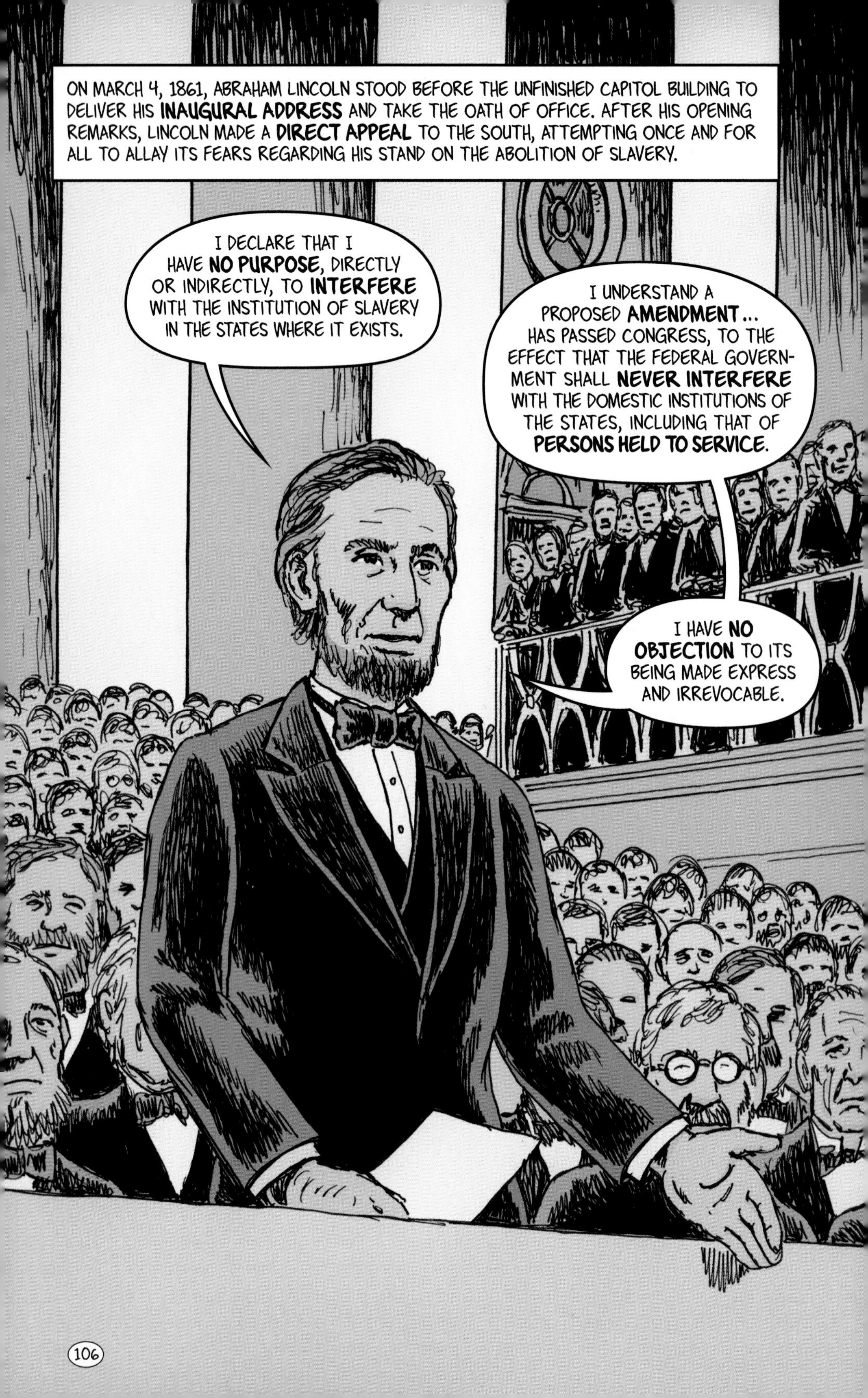
ON MARCH 4, 1861, ABRAHAM LINCOLN STOOD BEFORE THE UNFINISHED CAPITOL BUILDING TO DELIVER HIS **INAUGURAL ADDRESS** AND TAKE THE OATH OF OFFICE. AFTER HIS OPENING REMARKS, LINCOLN MADE A **DIRECT APPEAL** TO THE SOUTH, ATTEMPTING ONCE AND FOR ALL TO ALLAY ITS FEARS REGARDING HIS STAND ON THE ABOLITION OF SLAVERY.
I DECLARE THAT I HAVE **NO PURPOSE**, DIRECTLY OR INDIRECTLY, TO **INTERFERE** WITH THE INSTITUTION OF SLAVERY IN THE STATES WHERE IT EXISTS.
I UNDERSTAND A PROPOSED **AMENDMENT**... HAS PASSED CONGRESS, TO THE EFFECT THAT THE FEDERAL GOVERNMENT SHALL **NEVER INTERFERE** WITH THE DOMESTIC INSTITUTIONS OF THE STATES, INCLUDING THAT OF **PERSONS HELD TO SERVICE**.
I HAVE **NO OBJECTION** TO ITS BEING MADE EXPRESS AND IRREVOCABLE.

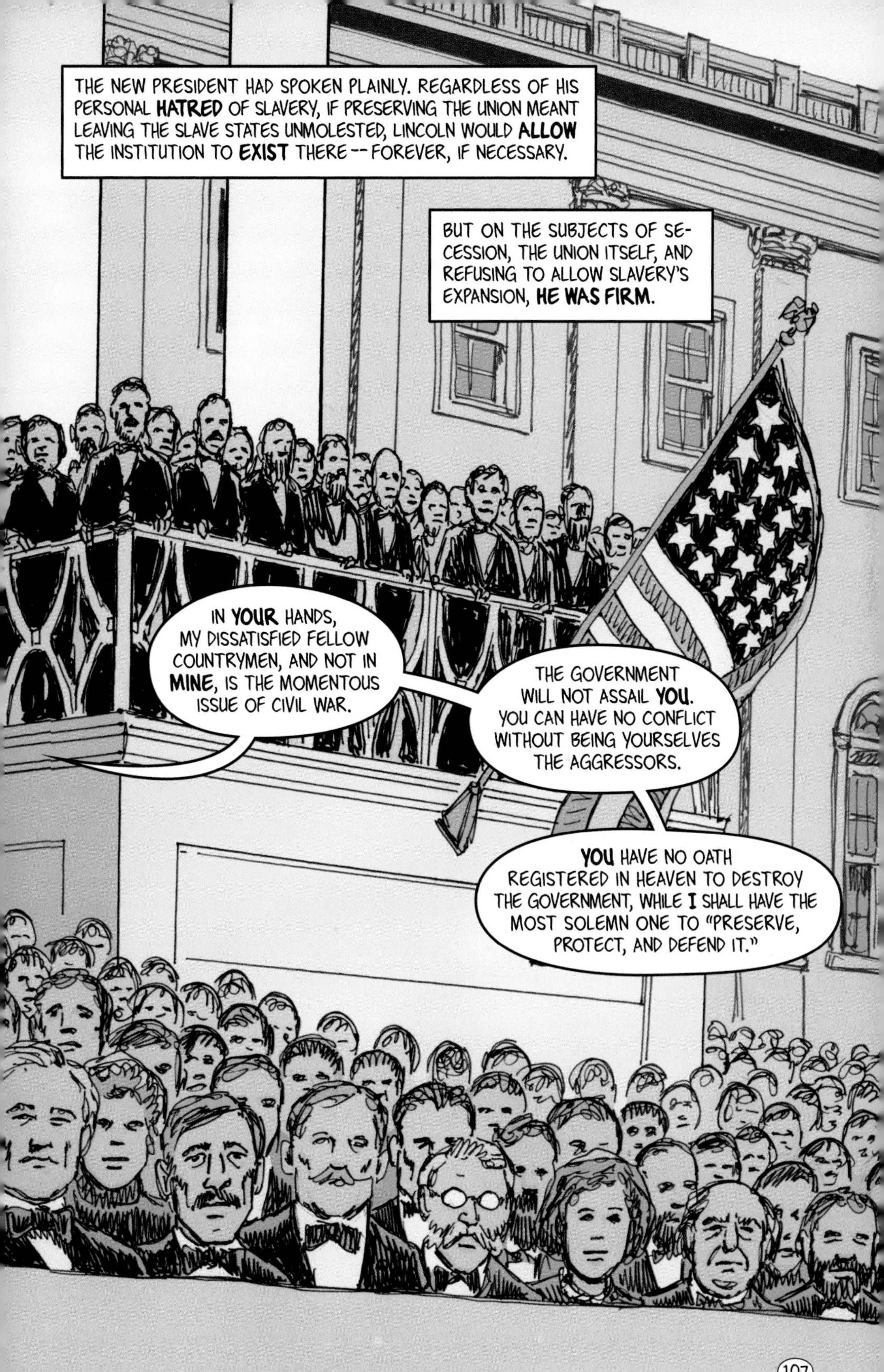
THE NEW PRESIDENT HAD SPOKEN PLAINLY. REGARDLESS OF HIS PERSONAL **HATRED** OF SLAVERY, IF PRESERVING THE UNION MEANT LEAVING THE SLAVE STATES UNMOLESTED, LINCOLN WOULD **ALLOW** THE INSTITUTION TO **EXIST** THERE--FOREVER, IF NECESSARY.
BUT ON THE SUBJECTS OF SECESSION, THE UNION ITSELF, AND REFUSING TO ALLOW SLAVERY'S EXPANSION, **HE WAS FIRM.**
IN **YOUR** HANDS, MY DISSATISFIED FELLOW COUNTRYMEN, AND NOT IN **MINE**, IS THE MOMENTOUS ISSUE OF CIVIL WAR.
THE GOVERNMENT WILL NOT ASSAIL **YOU**. YOU CAN HAVE NO CONFLICT WITHOUT BEING YOURSELVES THE AGGRESSORS.
YOU HAVE NO OATH REGISTERED IN HEAVEN TO DESTROY THE GOVERNMENT, WHILE **I** SHALL HAVE THE MOST SOLEMN ONE TO "PRESERVE, PROTECT, AND DEFEND IT."

STATES COULD STILL ABOLISH SLAVERY, IF THEY SO CHOSE. AND LINCOLN BELIEVED THEY **WOULD** IF IT COULD NOT BE EXPANDED. ON MARCH 16, 1861, HE SENT ALL STATE GOVERNORS A COPY OF THE CORWIN AMENDMENT.

LINCOLN'S **WORDS** AND ACTIONS WERE MEANT TO KEEP THE UNION TOGETHER, ALLOWING SLAVE STATES TO CONTINUE AS BEFORE IF THEY DID NOT SECEDE. FREDERICK DOUGLASS FELT **BETRAYED.**

WHAT AN EXCELLENT **SLAVE HOUND** HE IS!

THE REPUBLICAN PRESIDENT BENDS THE KNEE TO SLAVERY AS READILY AS ANY OF HIS **INFAMOUS PREDECESSORS.**

BUT THE CORWIN AMENDMENT WOULD NEVER BECOME PART OF THE U.S. CONSTITUTION. ON APRIL 12, 1861, CONFEDERATE FORCES FIRED ON FORT SUMTER.

THE **CIVIL WAR** HAD BEGUN.

[TO THIS DAY, THE AMENDMENT REMAINS ON THE BOOKS, UNRATIFIED.]

BOOM!!

DOUGLASS BECAME SO **DISTRESSED** OVER LINCOLN'S POSITION THAT HE MADE PLANS TO **EMIGRATE** TO HAITI.

THE FIRING ON FORT SUMTER CAUSED HIM TO CHANGE HIS PLANS.

WE ARE AT WAR! I MUST **STAY.**

LINCOLN CALLS FOR VOLUNTEERS

LINCOLN CALLED FOR 75,000 VOLUNTEERS TO SERVE 90-DAY ENLISTMENTS -- THEN THE LEGAL MAXIMUM -- TO **FIGHT** THE SECESSIONISTS. HE RECEIVED AN OVERWHELMING RESPONSE FROM PATRIOTIC NORTHERN CITIZENS, WHO BELIEVED THE WHOLE AFFAIR WOULD BE **OVER** IN JUST A FEW WEEKS, CERTAINLY **LESS** THAN THREE MONTHS.

THAT LINCOLN WOULD GO TO **WAR** AGAINST THE SLAVE STATES THRILLED FREDERICK DOUGLASS. WHAT **ANGERED** HIM WAS THAT NEGRO MEN WERE NOT ALLOWED TO ENLIST IN THE UNION ARMY.

IF THIS CONFLICT SHALL **EXPAND** TO THE GRAND DIMENSIONS WHICH EVENTS SEEM TO INDICATE, THE **IRON ARM** OF THE BLACK MAN MAY BE CALLED INTO SERVICE.

LET'S NOT ONLY BE **READY** ON CALL, BUT BE CASTING ABOUT FOR AN **OPPORTUNITY** TO STRIKE FOR THE **FREEDOM** OF THE SLAVE, AND FOR THE **RIGHTS** OF HUMAN NATURE.

LET A FEW **COLORED REGIMENTS** GO DOWN SOUTH AND ASSIST IN SETTING THEIR BROTHERS FREE, AND THEY COULD AND WOULD DO THIS WORK EFFECTIVELY FOR OUR GOVERNMENT.

THAT OPPORTUNITY CAME SOONER THAN EXPECTED.

DESPITE THE FALL OF FORT SUMTER, THE FEDERAL GOVERNMENT STILL HELD A NUMBER OF **STRATEGIC FORTS** ON THE CONFEDERATE COAST. ONE OF THEM WAS **FORT MONROE, VIRGINIA**, LOCATED AT THE MOUTH OF CHESAPEAKE BAY. **MAJOR GENERAL BENJAMIN BUTLER** WAS ITS COMMANDER. WHEN THREE ESCAPED SLAVES ARRIVED AT THE FORT, HE GAVE THEM **REFUGE** AND PUT THEM TO WORK ON THE FORTIFICATIONS.

AN AGENT FOR THE SLAVES' OWNERS DEMANDED THEIR RETURN, BASED ON THE **FUGITIVE SLAVE ACT**. BUT BUTLER WAS A **LAWYER**, AND HE RESPONDED AS ONE.

VIRGINIA HAS SECEDED AND CLAIMS TO BE A FOREIGN COUNTRY. I AM UNDER NO CONSTITUTIONAL OBLIGATIONS TO A FOREIGN COUNTRY.

BUT LINCOLN **DENIES** THE RIGHT OF SECESSION, SO WE ALL MUST **OBEY** FEDERAL LAWS. UNDER THE FUGITIVE SLAVE ACT, YOU MUST RETURN TO ME THOSE SLAVES.

BUT YOU **HAVE** SECEDED ANYWAY, AND THEREFORE CANNOT ASK TO BE COVERED BY THE LAWS OF THE UNION YOU **DEFY**. I HAVE THE RIGHT TO **KEEP** THESE SLAVES AS **"CONTRABAND OF WAR."** *

* The term meant **GOODS** or **PROPERTY** taken from those fighting for the opposing force.

BUTLER'S QUICK AND CLEVER THINKING PROVIDED AN **EXCUSE** FOR UNION OFFICERS TO KEEP AND PROTECT **ESCAPED SLAVES**. WITHIN WEEKS, BUTLER ALONE HAD MORE THAN A **THOUSAND** MEN, WOMEN, AND CHILDREN "CONTRABANDS" WITHIN HIS PROTECTION.

ON AUGUST 6, 1861, CONGRESS FORMALLY LEGALIZED BUTLER'S ACTION BY PASSING THE **FIRST CONFISCATION ACT**. THIS ALLOWED FOR THE SEIZURE OF **ANY PROPERTY**, INCLUDING SLAVES, USED TO **SUPPORT** THE **REBELLION** DURING THE WAR.

KILL THEM YANKEE-LOVERS! THEN BURN THE FARM TO THE GROUND!

DEATH TO THE UNION!

MISSOURI WAS ONE OF FOUR SLAVE STATES THAT REMAINED IN THE UNION -- ALONG WITH KENTUCKY, MARYLAND, AND DELAWARE. AND IT BECAME A BATTLE-GROUND FOR SOME OF THE WORST GUERRILLA FIGHTING IN THE WAR.

JOHN C. FRÉMONT WAS NOW A MAJOR GENERAL AND COMMANDER OF THE **UNION'S WESTERN FORCES**, HEADQUARTERED IN ST. LOUIS.

WITH MISSOURI PLUNGING INTO ANARCHY, HE KNEW HE HAD TO ACT **BOLDLY**.

THE REBELS' CAMPAIGN OF TERROR MUST STOP!

ON AUGUST 30, 1861, FRÉMONT PROCLAIMED **MARTIAL LAW**, ANNOUNCING THAT CIVILIANS BEARING ARMS AGAINST THE UNION WOULD BE COURT-MARTIALED AND SHOT IF CONVICTED, AND THAT ALL SLAVES OF THOSE AIDING THE REBELLION "ARE HEREBY DECLARED FREE MEN."

IN DOING THIS, FRÉMONT **TRANSFORMED** THE WAR FROM A FIGHT TO PRESERVE THE UNION INTO A CONFLICT FOR **UNIVERSAL FREEDOM**.

THIS WILL TEACH THE REBELS!

FRÉMONT FREES SLAVES IN MISSOURI

LIKE THE REST OF THE NATION, LINCOLN **DISCOVERED** WHAT FRÉMONT HAD DONE WHEN HE READ ABOUT IT IN THE NEXT DAY'S **NEWSPAPER**.

HE WAS NOT HAPPY.

THE GENERAL HAS DONE...

...WHAT?

FRÉMONT MAY HAVE WANTED A SOCIAL REVOLUTION, BUT LINCOLN DID NOT -- AT LEAST **NOT YET**.

LINCOLN HAD TO REIN IN HIS POLITICALLY POWERFUL GENERAL BEFORE THINGS GOT COMPLETELY OUT OF HAND. HE QUICKLY WROTE A **CONFIDENTIAL LETTER**.

Two points in your proclamation of August 30 give me some anxiety. First. Should you shoot a man, according to the proclamation, the Confederates would very certainly shoot our best men in their hands in retaliation; and so, man for man, indefinitely.

It is, therefore, my order that you allow no man to be shot under the proclamation without first having my approbation or consent.

Second. I think there is great danger that the closing paragraph, in relation to the confiscation of property and the liberating slaves of traitorous owners, will alarm our Southern Union friends and turn them against us; perhaps ruin our rather fair prospect for Kentucky.

LINCOLN THEN ASKED FRÉMONT TO "AS OF YOUR OWN MOTION" **MODIFY** HIS PROCLAMATION TO BRING IT IN LINE WITH THE FIRST CONFISCATION ACT.

WHEN HE RECEIVED LINCOLN'S LETTER, FRÉMONT WAS **FURIOUS**.

IF LINCOLN WANTS A PUBLIC RETRACTION, LET **HIM** DO IT!

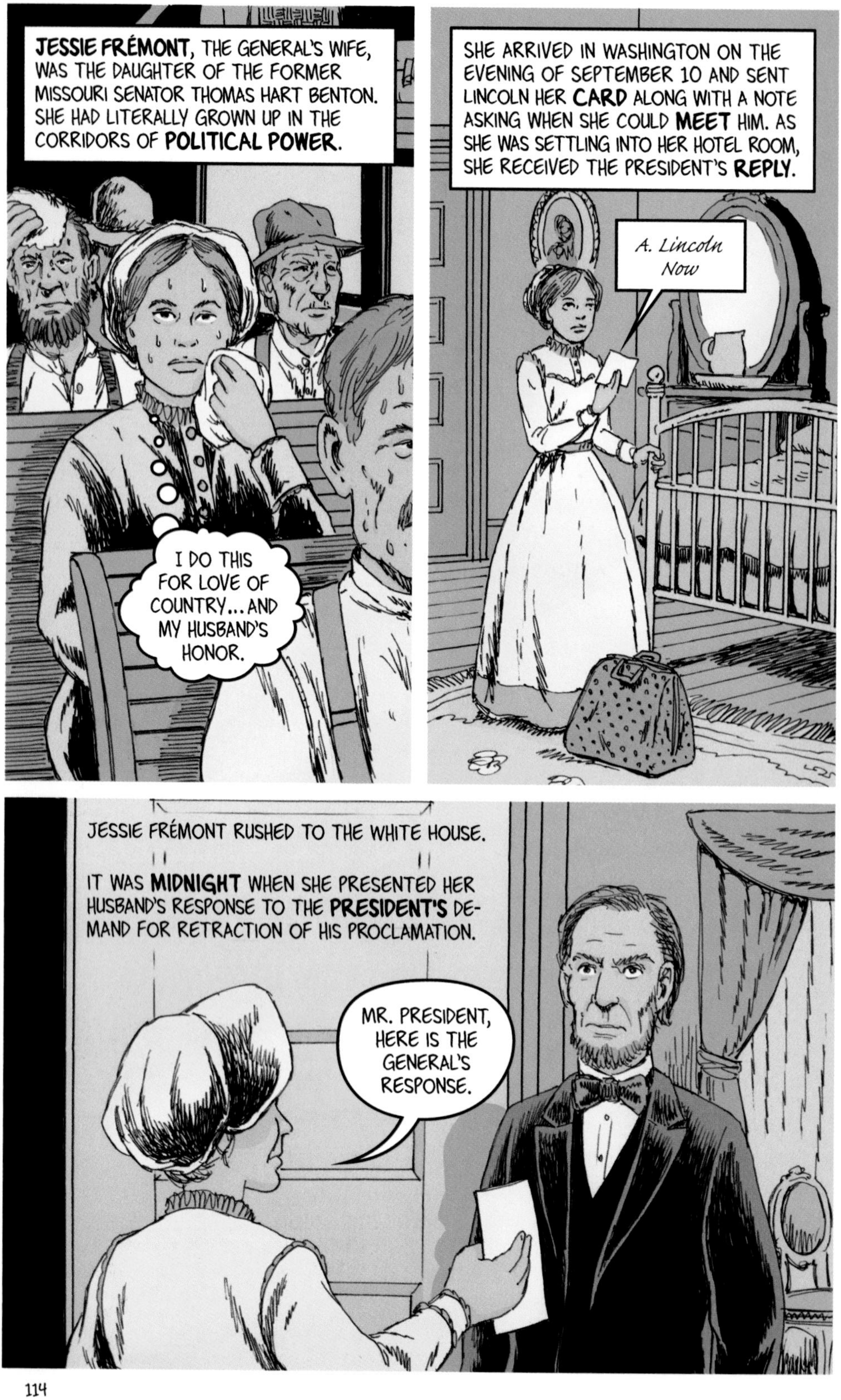
JESSIE FRÉMONT, THE GENERAL'S WIFE, WAS THE DAUGHTER OF THE FORMER MISSOURI SENATOR THOMAS HART BENTON. SHE HAD LITERALLY GROWN UP IN THE CORRIDORS OF POLITICAL POWER.
I DO THIS FOR LOVE OF COUNTRY... AND MY HUSBAND'S HONOR.
SHE ARRIVED IN WASHINGTON ON THE EVENING OF SEPTEMBER 10 AND SENT LINCOLN HER CARD ALONG WITH A NOTE ASKING WHEN SHE COULD MEET HIM. AS SHE WAS SETTLING INTO HER HOTEL ROOM, SHE RECEIVED THE PRESIDENT'S REPLY.
A. Lincoln Now
JESSIE FRÉMONT RUSHED TO THE WHITE HOUSE.
IT WAS MIDNIGHT WHEN SHE PRESENTED HER HUSBAND'S RESPONSE TO THE PRESIDENT'S DEMAND FOR RETRACTION OF HIS PROCLAMATION.
MR. PRESIDENT, HERE IS THE GENERAL'S RESPONSE.

GENERAL FRÉMONT WROTE, IN PART, "IF I WERE TO RETRACT OF MY OWN ACCORD, IT WOULD IMPLY THAT I MYSELF THOUGHT IT WRONG, AND THAT I HAD ACTED WITHOUT THE REFLECTION WHICH THE GRAVITY OF THE POINT DEMANDED. BUT I DID NOT."

THE MAN HAD **GALL,** DARING THE PRESIDENT TO PUBLICLY RESCIND THE PROCLAMATION, KNOWING IT WOULD INFURIATE THE POWERFUL **ANTI-SLAVERY WING** OF THE REPUBLICAN PARTY.

I HAVE WRITTEN TO THE GENERAL, AND HE KNOWS WHAT I WANT DONE.

THE GENERAL FEELS HE IS AT THE GREAT DISADVANTAGE OF BEING OPPOSED BY PEOPLE IN WHOM YOU HAVE EVERY CONFIDENCE.

WHOM DO YOU MEAN?

THE GENERAL'S CONVICTION IS THAT IT WILL BE LONG AND DREADFUL WORK TO CONQUER BY ARMS ALONE, THAT THERE MUST BE OTHER CONSIDERATION TO GET US THE SUPPORT OF FOREIGN COUNTRIES...

AND HE IS ALSO AWARE, AS YOU ARE, THAT ENGLAND, FRANCE, AND SPAIN ARE THINKING OF RECOGNIZING THE SOUTH... ENGLAND BECAUSE OF HER COTTON INTERESTS, AND FRANCE BECAUSE THE EMPEROR DISLIKES US.

YOU ARE **QUITE** A **FEMALE** POLITICIAN.

HE MEANT IT AS AN **INSULT.** THIS WAS A TIME WHEN WOMEN COULD NOT VOTE AND **POLITICS** WAS CONSIDERED MEN'S WORK. LINCOLN WAS TELLING MRS. FRÉMONT TO MIND HER OWN BUSINESS.

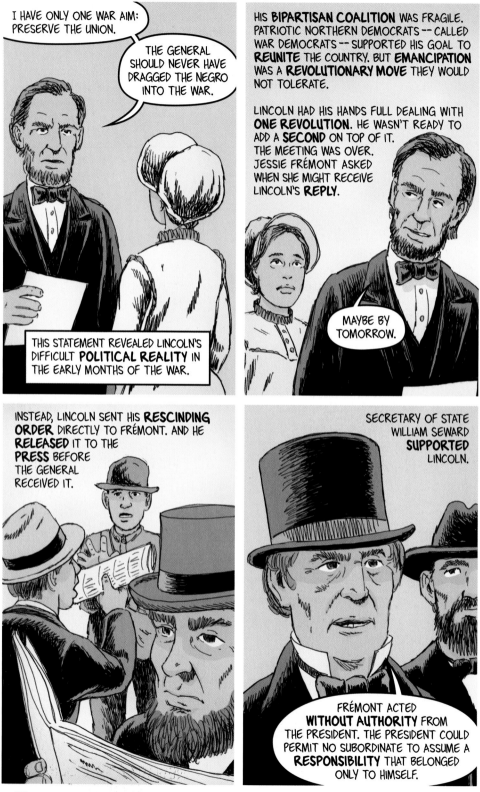

I HAVE ONLY ONE WAR AIM: PRESERVE THE UNION.

THE GENERAL SHOULD NEVER HAVE DRAGGED THE NEGRO INTO THE WAR.

HIS **BIPARTISAN COALITION** WAS FRAGILE. PATRIOTIC NORTHERN DEMOCRATS -- CALLED WAR DEMOCRATS -- SUPPORTED HIS GOAL TO **REUNITE** THE COUNTRY. BUT **EMANCIPATION** WAS A **REVOLUTIONARY MOVE** THEY WOULD NOT TOLERATE.

LINCOLN HAD HIS HANDS FULL DEALING WITH **ONE REVOLUTION.** HE WASN'T READY TO ADD A **SECOND** ON TOP OF IT. THE MEETING WAS OVER. JESSIE FRÉMONT ASKED WHEN SHE MIGHT RECEIVE LINCOLN'S **REPLY.**

MAYBE BY TOMORROW.

THIS STATEMENT REVEALED LINCOLN'S DIFFICULT **POLITICAL REALITY** IN THE EARLY MONTHS OF THE WAR.

INSTEAD, LINCOLN SENT HIS **RESCINDING ORDER** DIRECTLY TO FRÉMONT. AND HE **RELEASED** IT TO THE **PRESS** BEFORE THE GENERAL RECEIVED IT.

SECRETARY OF STATE WILLIAM SEWARD **SUPPORTED** LINCOLN.

FRÉMONT ACTED **WITHOUT AUTHORITY** FROM THE PRESIDENT. THE PRESIDENT COULD PERMIT NO SUBORDINATE TO ASSUME A **RESPONSIBILITY** THAT BELONGED ONLY TO HIMSELF.

FREDERICK DOUGLASS **RESPONDED** WITH BITTER **DISAPPOINTMENT** TO LINCOLN'S ORDER RESCINDING FRÉMONT'S PROCLAMATION.

DOUGLASS COULD NOT UNDERSTAND WHY THE NORTH STILL **REFUSED** TO **ENLIST** NEGROES IN THEIR ARMY. AS HE POINTED OUT IN SEPTEMBER 1861, THE **CONFEDERATES** WERE ALREADY DOING IT.

THERE ARE AT THE PRESENT MOMENT MANY **COLORED MEN** IN THE **CONFEDERATE ARMY** DOING DUTY...

...AS REAL SOLDIERS.

THE WEAKNESS AND **IMBECILITY** OF THE LETTER OF THE PRESIDENT, CONDEMNING THAT PROCLAMATION, HAVE CHARAC- TERIZED THE WHOLE WAR.

PRESIDENT, GOVERNMENT, AND ARMY STAND **PARALYZED** IN THE PRESENCE OF SLAVERY.

DOUGLASS WAS RESTATING **REPORTS** FROM NEWSPAPERS. THE TRUTH WAS THAT SOME OFFICERS BROUGHT THEIR PERSONAL SERVANTS AND COOKS WITH THEM. ONE SUCH SLAVE WAS **WILLIAM MACK LEE**, GENERAL ROBERT E. LEE'S PERSONAL COOK.

HISTORIANS WOULD LATER DETERMINE THE REPORTS OF CONFEDERATE NEGRO UNITS TO BE AN **EXAGGERATION**...

...POSSIBLY CAUSED BY NORTHERN RE- PORTERS SEEING FROM A DISTANCE THE **GUNPOWDER-BLACKENED FACES** OF SOME CONFEDERATE SOLDIERS.

OTHERS WERE **HIRED** FROM LOCAL WHITE MASTERS TO PERFORM A VARIETY OF CAMP AND FIELD DUTIES, LIKE BUILDING TEMPORARY FORTIFICATIONS.

117

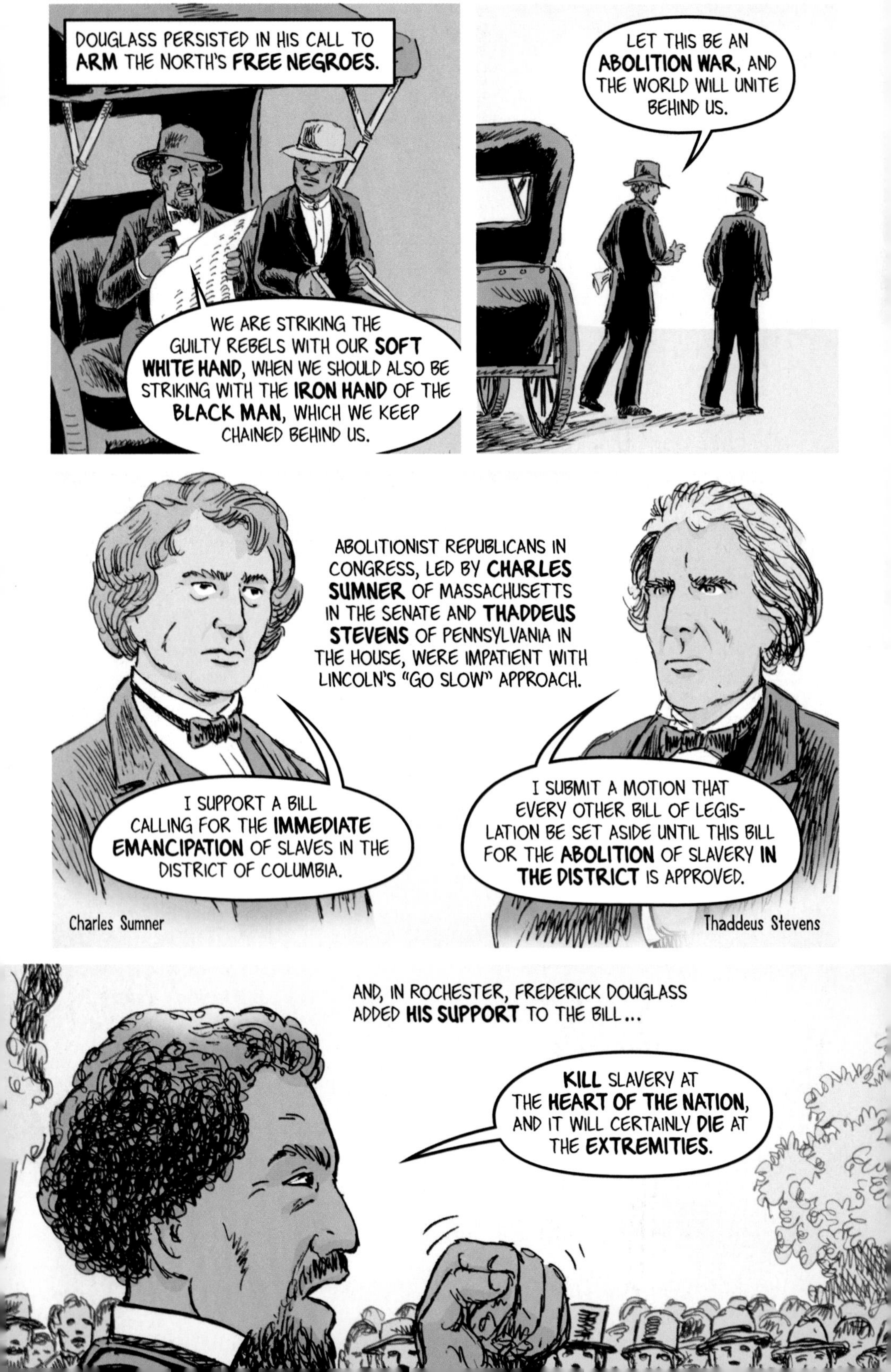
DOUGLASS PERSISTED IN HIS CALL TO **ARM** THE NORTH'S **FREE NEGROES**.
WE ARE STRIKING THE GUILTY REBELS WITH OUR **SOFT WHITE HAND**, WHEN WE SHOULD ALSO BE STRIKING WITH THE **IRON HAND** OF THE **BLACK MAN**, WHICH WE KEEP CHAINED BEHIND US.
LET THIS BE AN **ABOLITION WAR**, AND THE WORLD WILL UNITE BEHIND US.
ABOLITIONIST REPUBLICANS IN CONGRESS, LED BY **CHARLES SUMNER** OF MASSACHUSETTS IN THE SENATE AND **THADDEUS STEVENS** OF PENNSYLVANIA IN THE HOUSE, WERE IMPATIENT WITH LINCOLN'S "GO SLOW" APPROACH.
I SUPPORT A BILL CALLING FOR THE **IMMEDIATE EMANCIPATION** OF SLAVES IN THE DISTRICT OF COLUMBIA.
I SUBMIT A MOTION THAT EVERY OTHER BILL OF LEGISLATION BE SET ASIDE UNTIL THIS BILL FOR THE **ABOLITION** OF SLAVERY **IN THE DISTRICT** IS APPROVED.
Charles Sumner
Thaddeus Stevens
AND, IN ROCHESTER, FREDERICK DOUGLASS ADDED **HIS SUPPORT** TO THE BILL...
KILL SLAVERY AT THE **HEART OF THE NATION**, AND IT WILL CERTAINLY **DIE** AT THE **EXTREMITIES**.

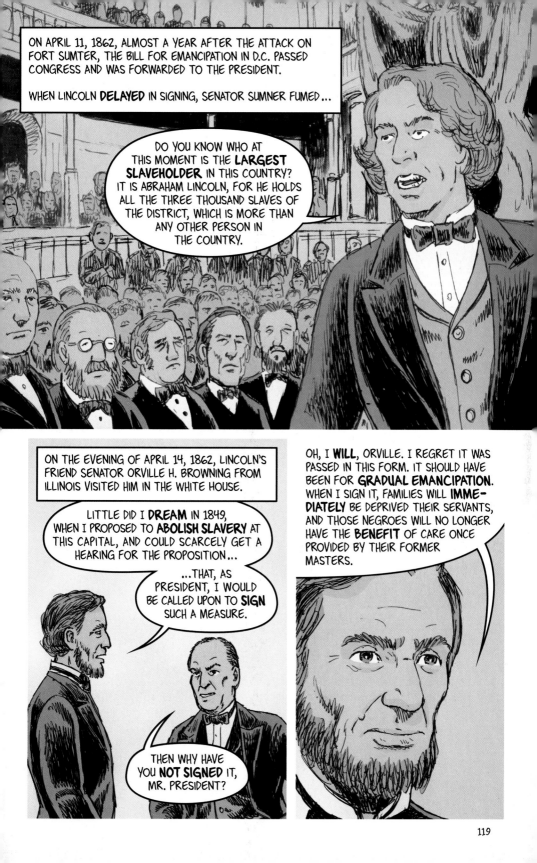

ON APRIL 11, 1862, ALMOST A YEAR AFTER THE ATTACK ON FORT SUMTER, THE BILL FOR EMANCIPATION IN D.C. PASSED CONGRESS AND WAS FORWARDED TO THE PRESIDENT.

WHEN LINCOLN **DELAYED** IN SIGNING, SENATOR SUMNER FUMED...

DO YOU KNOW WHO AT THIS MOMENT IS THE **LARGEST SLAVEHOLDER** IN THIS COUNTRY? IT IS ABRAHAM LINCOLN, FOR HE HOLDS ALL THE THREE THOUSAND SLAVES OF THE DISTRICT, WHICH IS MORE THAN ANY OTHER PERSON IN THE COUNTRY.

ON THE EVENING OF APRIL 14, 1862, LINCOLN'S FRIEND SENATOR ORVILLE H. BROWNING FROM ILLINOIS VISITED HIM IN THE WHITE HOUSE.

LITTLE DID I **DREAM** IN 1849, WHEN I PROPOSED TO **ABOLISH SLAVERY** AT THIS CAPITAL, AND COULD SCARCELY GET A HEARING FOR THE PROPOSITION...

...THAT, AS PRESIDENT, I WOULD BE CALLED UPON TO **SIGN** SUCH A MEASURE.

THEN WHY HAVE YOU **NOT SIGNED** IT, MR. PRESIDENT?

OH, I **WILL**, ORVILLE. I REGRET IT WAS PASSED IN THIS FORM. IT SHOULD HAVE BEEN FOR **GRADUAL EMANCIPATION**. WHEN I SIGN IT, FAMILIES WILL **IMMEDIATELY** BE DEPRIVED THEIR SERVANTS, AND THOSE NEGROES WILL NO LONGER HAVE THE **BENEFIT** OF CARE ONCE PROVIDED BY THEIR FORMER MASTERS.

THE **REASON** FOR MY DELAY IS THAT CHARLES WICKLIFFE* HAS TWO FAMILY SERVANTS, SLAVES, WITH HIM HERE WHO ARE **SICKLY.**

IMMEDIATE FREEDOM WOULD MORE **HURT** THAN HELP THEM. HE COULD NOT GET THEM OUT OF THE DISTRICT UNTIL WEDNESDAY, AND CAME TO ME AND ASKED FOR TIME TO DO SO. I **AGREED.**

I MUST ASK YOU TO KEEP THIS INFORMATION CONFIDENTIAL.

*Congressman from Kentucky.

THEN, ON THE AFTERNOON OF WEDNESDAY, APRIL 16, 1862, PRESIDENT ABRAHAM LINCOLN SIGNED THE DISTRICT'S EMANCIPATION ACT INTO **LAW.**

INCLUDED IN ITS PROVISIONS WAS **COMPENSATION** OF UP TO $300 PER FREED SLAVE TO FORMER OWNERS LOYAL TO THE UNION. A TOTAL OF 930 SUCH PETITIONS, COVERING 2,989 FORMER SLAVES, WERE SUBMITTED.

HURRAH!

THOUGH LINCOLN RECOGNIZED THE RAPIDLY RISING **STRENGTH** OF THE ABOLITION MOVEMENT, HE WAS NOT YET CONVINCED IT HAD REACHED THE **TIPPING POINT.** HIS QUESTION REMAINED...

WHAT NEXT?

120

THIS WAS NOT LINCOLN'S ONLY ATTEMPT TO MANAGE EVENTS THREATENING TO OVERWHELM HIM AND THE NATION.

FOR MONTHS, HE HAD TRIED TO CONVINCE THE FOUR SLAVE STATES STILL IN THE UNION TO ACCEPT **GRADUAL** AND **COMPENSATED EMANCIPATION.** ON JULY 12, 1862, HE MADE A LAST APPEAL TO THEIR REPRESENTATIVES.

GENTLEMEN... I DO NOT SPEAK OF EMANCIPATION **AT ONCE**, BUT OF A **DECISION** AT ONCE TO EMANCIPATE **GRADUALLY.**

BY **CONCEDING** WHAT I NOW ASK, YOU CAN RELIEVE ME, AND MUCH MORE, CAN RELIEVE THE **COUNTRY**, IN THIS IMPORTANT POINT.

BEFORE YOU **ADJOURN** AND LEAVE THE CAPITAL FOR SUMMER RECESS... CONSIDER AND **DISCUSS** THIS AMONG YOURSELVES.

OUR COMMON COUNTRY IS IN GREAT **PERIL**, DEMANDING THE LOFTIEST VIEWS AND BOLDEST **ACTION** TO BRING IT SPEEDY RELIEF. ONCE RELIEVED, ITS FORM OF GOVERNMENT IS SAVED TO THE WORLD...

...AND ITS **HAPPY FUTURE** FULLY ASSURED.

A FEW DAYS LATER, LINCOLN HAD HIS ANSWER...

MR. CHASE, THE BORDER STATE REPRESENTATIVES HAVE **REJECTED** MY PLEA.

THEIR REASONS?

ARE LONG AND LEGALISTIC. AND...UNFORTUNATELY... AS I EXPECTED.

121

LINCOLN DID HAVE CONGRESSIONAL SUPPORT ON **ANOTHER EFFORT** REGARDING THE FUTURE OF FREED SLAVES -- **COLONIZATION.** THE HOUSE OF REPRESENTATIVES **SELECT COMMITTEE ON EMANCIPATION AND COLONIZATION** APPROPRIATED $600,000 FOR HIS USE ON THAT ISSUE.

AMONG THE PROPOSALS HE WAS CONSIDERING WAS A COLONY IN THE **CHIRIQUÍ PROVINCE** NEAR PANAMA.

ON AUGUST 14, 1862, HE SUMMONED A GROUP OF FIVE LEADERS OF THE NEGRO COMMUNITY IN WASHINGTON, D.C., TO DISCUSS THE MATTER.

Edward M. Thompson

John T. Costin

John F. Cook

Benjamin McCoy

Cornelius Clark

IT WAS A HISTORIC OCCASION. FOR THE FIRST TIME **FREE AFRICAN AMERICANS** WHO WERE NOT SERVANTS WERE **MEETING** THE PRESIDENT.

GENTLEMEN, THANK YOU FOR COMING TO SEE ME.

YOUR RACE IS SUFFERING... THE GREATEST WRONG INFLICTED ON ANY PEOPLE. BUT, EVEN WHEN YOU CEASE TO BE SLAVES, YOU ARE NOT PLACED ON AN EQUAL BASIS WITH THE WHITE RACE.

IT IS NOT RIGHT, BUT IT IS A FACT WITH WHICH WE HAVE TO DEAL.

LINCOLN THEN WENT ON TO DESCRIBE HIS COL-
ONIZATION OFFER, MENTIONING COLONIES IN
LIBERIA IN AFRICA AND LOCATIONS IN CENTRAL
AMERICA, AND SAID THAT THE GOVERNMENT
WOULD PAY TRAVEL AND OTHER EXPENSES
TO ASSIST ANY WHO WISHED TO GO.

MR. PRESIDENT, WE
WILL HOLD A CONSULTATION
AND IN A SHORT TIME GIVE
YOU AN ANSWER.

TAKE YOUR
FULL TIME -- NO HURRY
AT ALL.

I WANT YOU
TO LET ME KNOW
WHETHER THIS
CAN BE DONE
OR NOT.

IRONICALLY, ABOUT A MONTH EARLIER,
LINCOLN HAD SECRETLY FORMULATED A
PLAN THAT WOULD ACTUALLY **ELIMINATE**
ANY SUPPORT FOR COLONIZATION.

ON JULY 13, 1862, HE TOLD SECRETARY OF
STATE WILLIAM SEWARD AND SECRETARY OF
THE NAVY GIDEON WELLES THAT HE HAD...

...COME TO
THE CONCLUSION THAT
WE MUST **FREE**
THE SLAVES.

THE SECRETARIES WERE **STUNNED**. LINCOLN'S WORDS WERE NOTHING LESS THAN A
COMPLETE **SHIFT** IN HIS POLICY ON THE WAR. WHAT HAD CAUSED SUCH A **CHANGE**?

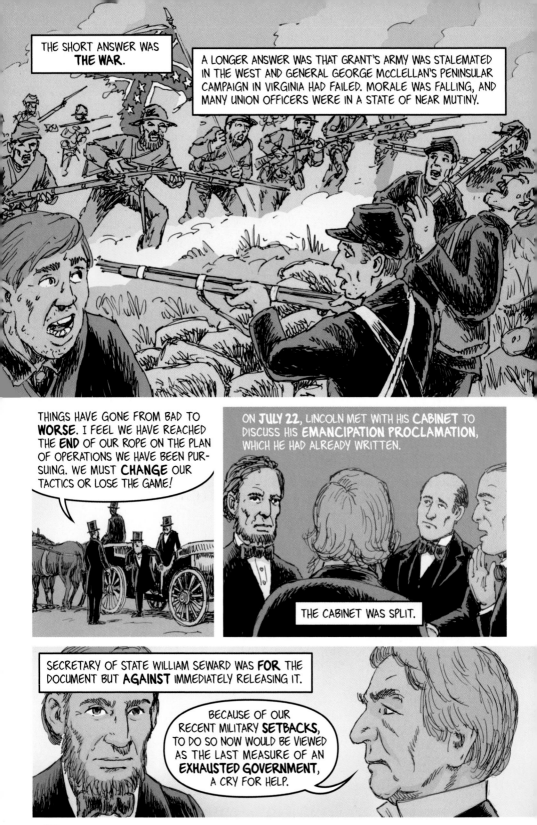

THE SHORT ANSWER WAS **THE WAR.**

A LONGER ANSWER WAS THAT GRANT'S ARMY WAS STALEMATED IN THE WEST AND GENERAL GEORGE MCCLELLAN'S PENINSULAR CAMPAIGN IN VIRGINIA HAD FAILED. MORALE WAS FALLING, AND MANY UNION OFFICERS WERE IN A STATE OF NEAR MUTINY.

THINGS HAVE GONE FROM BAD TO **WORSE.** I FEEL WE HAVE REACHED THE **END** OF OUR ROPE ON THE PLAN OF OPERATIONS WE HAVE BEEN PUR- SUING. WE MUST **CHANGE** OUR TACTICS OR LOSE THE GAME!

ON **JULY 22,** LINCOLN MET WITH HIS **CABINET** TO DISCUSS HIS **EMANCIPATION PROCLAMATION,** WHICH HE HAD ALREADY WRITTEN.

THE CABINET WAS SPLIT.

SECRETARY OF STATE WILLIAM SEWARD WAS **FOR** THE DOCUMENT BUT **AGAINST** IMMEDIATELY RELEASING IT.

BECAUSE OF OUR RECENT MILITARY **SETBACKS,** TO DO SO NOW WOULD BE VIEWED AS THE LAST MEASURE OF AN **EXHAUSTED GOVERNMENT,** A CRY FOR HELP.

SWAYED BY SEWARD'S REASONING, LINCOLN AGREED TO **DELAY** AN ANNOUNCEMENT UNTIL AFTER A UNION **VICTORY**.

IN ADDITION, HE TOLD HIS CABINET THAT THE PROCLAMATION MUST BE KEPT SECRET UNTIL HE MADE HIS ANNOUNCEMENT. SO DURING THIS PERIOD, LINCOLN WAS KEEPING HIS OPTIONS FULLY OPEN, SIMULTANEOUSLY PURSUING TWO COMPLETELY DIFFERENT POLICIES.

OF COURSE, ABOLITIONISTS KNEW ONLY OF THE PUBLIC ONE -- AND THEY SURELY DIDN'T LIKE IT. THE NORTH'S NEGRO COMMUNITY OVERWHELMINGLY **REJECTED** THE COLONIZATION PLAN.

MR. LINCOLN IS SAYING, "I DON'T LIKE YOU, YOU MUST CLEAR OUT OF THE COUNTRY."

ON AUGUST 19, 1862, *THE NEW YORK TRIBUNE'S* EDITOR, **HORACE GREELEY**, WROTE AN EDITORIAL, "THE PRAYER OF TWENTY MILLIONS."

"WE THINK YOU ARE... DISASTROUSLY REMISS IN THE DISCHARGE OF YOUR...DUTY...

"AN IMMENSE MAJORITY OF... YOUR COUNTRYMEN REQUIRE...A FRANK...UNQUALIFIED...EXECUTION OF THE LAWS OF THE LAND... ESPECIALLY OF THE CONFISCATION ACT."

PERHAPS THIS WILL FORCE THE PRESIDENT TO **ACT**.

ON AUGUST 22, ABRAHAM LINCOLN WROTE A RESPONSE, WHICH GREELEY PUBLISHED.

Hon. Horace Greeley:

Dear Sir

I have just read your editorial addressed to me . . .

My paramount object in this struggle is to save the Union, and is *not either to save or destroy slavery*. If I could save the Union without freeing *any* slave I would do it, and if I could save it by freeing *all* the slaves I would do it; and if I could save it by *freeing some* and leaving others alone I would also do that.

What I *do about slavery*, and the colored race, I do because I believe it helps to *save the Union*; and what I forbear, I forbear because I do not believe it would help to save the Union . . .

THESE WERE CALLOUS, OFF-PUTTING WORDS TO ANY ABOLITIONIST. BUT DOUGLASS SAW IN LINCOLN'S CONCLUSION A HINT OF SOMETHING ELSE...

HE SAYS, "I INTEND NO MODIFICATION OF MY OFT-EXPRESSED **PERSONAL WISH** THAT **ALL MEN** EVERYWHERE COULD BE **FREE**."

THERE IS **YET HOPE...**

ON **SEPTEMBER 17, 1862**, IN MARYLAND, THE UNION ARMY OF THE POTOMAC **STOPPED** THE CONFEDERATE ARMY'S INVASION IN THE **BATTLE OF ANTIETAM**, FORCING THE CONFEDERATES TO **RETREAT** BACK TO VIRGINIA.

I THINK THE TIME HAS COME NOW. I WISH WE WERE IN BETTER CONDITION. BUT THE REBEL ARMY HAS BEEN DRIVEN OUT OF MARYLAND, AND PENNSYLVANIA IS NO LONGER IN DANGER OF INVASION.

... ALL PERSONS HELD AS SLAVES WITHIN ANY STATE, OR DESIGNATED PART OF A STATE, THE PEOPLE WHEREOF SHALL THEN BE IN REBELLION AGAINST THE UNITED STATES, SHALL BE THEN, THENCEFORWARD, AND FOREVER **FREE**...

LINCOLN'S **PRELIMINARY EMANCIPATION PROCLAMATION**, ANNOUNCED ON SEPTEMBER 22, 1862, HIT THE NATION LIKE A THUNDERBOLT.

THOUGH IT WOULD NOT GO INTO **EFFECT** UNTIL JANUARY 1, 1863, ANTI-SLAVERY ADVOCATES WERE **JUBILANT**.

LINCOLN HAD OFTEN DISAPPOINTED FREDERICK DOUGLASS, BUT HEARING THIS NEWS WAS THE **HAPPIEST MOMENT** IN DOUGLASS'S LIFE.

WE **SHOUT FOR JOY** THAT WE LIVE TO RECORD THIS **RIGHTEOUS DECREE**...

ABRAHAM LINCOLN WILL TAKE NO STEP BACKWARD... IF HE HAS TAUGHT US TO CONFIDE IN NOTHING ELSE, HE HAS TAUGHT US TO CONFIDE IN HIS WORD.

ON THE AFTERNOON OF JANUARY 1, 1863, LINCOLN SPENT HOURS SHAKING THE HANDS OF GUESTS AT THE WHITE HOUSE NEW YEAR'S DAY RECEPTION. THEN HE WENT UP TO HIS OFFICE, WHERE SECRETARY OF STATE SEWARD HAD THE **EMANCIPATION PROCLAMATION** READY FOR HIS SIGNATURE.

I NEVER, IN MY LIFE, FELT MORE CERTAIN THAT I WAS DOING RIGHT THAN I DO IN SIGNING THIS PAPER.

FREDERICK DOUGLASS WAS IN **BOSTON'S TREMONT TEMPLE,** HOME TO THE ABOLITIONIST CAUSE. TOGETHER WITH MORE THAN 3,000 PEOPLE, HE ANXIOUSLY AWAITED WORD OF LINCOLN'S SIGNATURE.

FOR MORE THAN 12 HOURS, THEY WAITED. THEN, JUST AFTER 11:00 P.M. ...

BLOW YE the TRUMPET, BLOW!... LET ALL the NATIONS KNOW... the YEAR of JUBILEE's COME!

IT IS COMING!

IT IS ON THE WIRES!

DOUGLASS STOOD UP AND LED THE CROWD IN A TRIUMPHANT RENDITION OF AN ABOLITIONIST ANTHEM FAVORED BY JOHN BROWN.

DOUGLASS PROMPTLY EMBARKED ON THE LECTURE CIRCUIT, POUNDING HOME THE **HISTORIC IMPACT** OF THE PROCLAMATION. THE SPEAKING SERIES CLIMAXED AT NEW YORK CITY'S COOPER UNION, THE NATION'S MOST PRESTIGIOUS LECTURE HALL, ON FEBRUARY 6, 1863.

WE ARE **ALL** LIBERATED BY THIS DOCUMENT.

BUT, DOUGLASS SAID, THE LIBERATION WOULD BE **INCOMPLETE** UNLESS BLACK UNITS WERE ALLOWED TO **FIGHT**.

THE COLORED MAN ONLY WAITS FOR HONORABLE **ADMISSION** INTO THE **SERVICE** OF THE COUNTRY.

I DON'T SAY THEY WILL FIGHT BETTER THAN OTHER MEN. I SAY... **GIVE THEM A CHANCE.**

THE PROGRESSIVE MASSACHUSETTS **GOVERNOR JOHN ANDREW** AGREED. BECAUSE THE EMANCIPATION PROCLAMATION AUTHORIZED THE ENLISTMENT OF BLACK SOLDIERS, ANDREW ASKED MAJOR GEORGE STEARNS -- A WEALTHY ABOLITIONIST -- TO ORGANIZE THE **54TH MASSACHUSETTS COLORED REGIMENT.**

WITH DOUGLASS'S HELP, MORE THAN 100 MEN FROM UPSTATE NEW YORK WERE RECRUITED INTO IT. AMONG THEM WERE DOUGLASS'S SONS **LEWIS** AND **CHARLES**.

THE 54TH MASSACHUSETTS BECAME ONE OF THE MOST **FAMOUS** UNION REGIMENTS IN THE WAR, ESTABLISHING ITS REPUTATION FOR **VALOR** IN THE BLOODY BATTLE OF FORT WAGNER, IN SOUTH CAROLINA.

BUT BLACK TROOPS FOUND THEMSELVES VICTIMS OF **UNEQUAL PAY**, UNEQUAL PROMOTION, AND OTHER ACTS OF **DISCRIMINATION**.

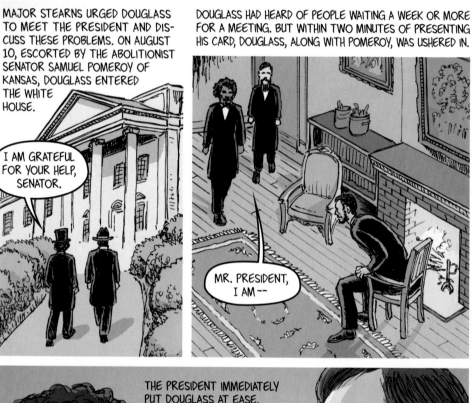

MAJOR STEARNS URGED DOUGLASS TO MEET THE PRESIDENT AND DISCUSS THESE PROBLEMS. ON AUGUST 10, ESCORTED BY THE ABOLITIONIST SENATOR SAMUEL POMEROY OF KANSAS, DOUGLASS ENTERED THE WHITE HOUSE.

I AM GRATEFUL FOR YOUR HELP, SENATOR.

DOUGLASS HAD HEARD OF PEOPLE WAITING A WEEK OR MORE FOR A MEETING. BUT WITHIN TWO MINUTES OF PRESENTING HIS CARD, DOUGLASS, ALONG WITH POMEROY, WAS USHERED IN.

MR. PRESIDENT, I AM --

THE PRESIDENT IMMEDIATELY PUT DOUGLASS AT EASE.

I KNOW WHO YOU ARE, MR. DOUGLASS. MR. SEWARD HAS TOLD ME ALL ABOUT YOU. I AM GLAD TO MEET YOU.

FREDERICK DOUGLASS LATER WROTE THAT WITH LINCOLN HE FELT HE WAS IN THE PRESENCE OF AN HONEST MAN DOING HIS BEST TO SAVE A NATION. THIS GAVE DOUGLASS THE COURAGE TO GET QUICKLY TO THE POINT.

MR. PRESIDENT, I HAVE HAD SOME SUCCESS IN RECRUITING COLORED TROOPS...

...BUT RECENTLY THE TASK HAS BECOME DIFFICULT.

BE SPECIFIC, MR. DOUGLASS.

THERE ARE THREE ISSUES. COLORED SOLDIERS SHOULD HAVE PAY EQUAL TO THAT OF WHITE SOLDIERS. PRESENTLY THEY DO NOT.

SECOND, PROMOTIONS, PARTICULARLY AS A RESULT OF VALOR IN COMBAT, SHOULD BE EQUAL AS WELL.

THIRD, JEFFERSON DAVIS HAS THREATENED TO EXECUTE ANY NEGRO SOLDIER CAPTURED BY THE CONFEDERATES. IF THIS THREAT IS CARRIED OUT, YOU NEED TO RETALIATE IN KIND.

MR. DOUGLASS, IT WAS WITH **GREAT DIFFICULTY** THAT I COULD GET THE COLORED SOLDIERS INTO THE ARMY AT ALL. YOU KNOW THE PREJUDICES EXISTING AGAINST THEM... IT WAS **NECESSARY** AT THE FIRST THAT WE SHOULD MAKE **SOME** DISCRIMINATION AGAINST THEM; THEY WERE **ON TRIAL.**

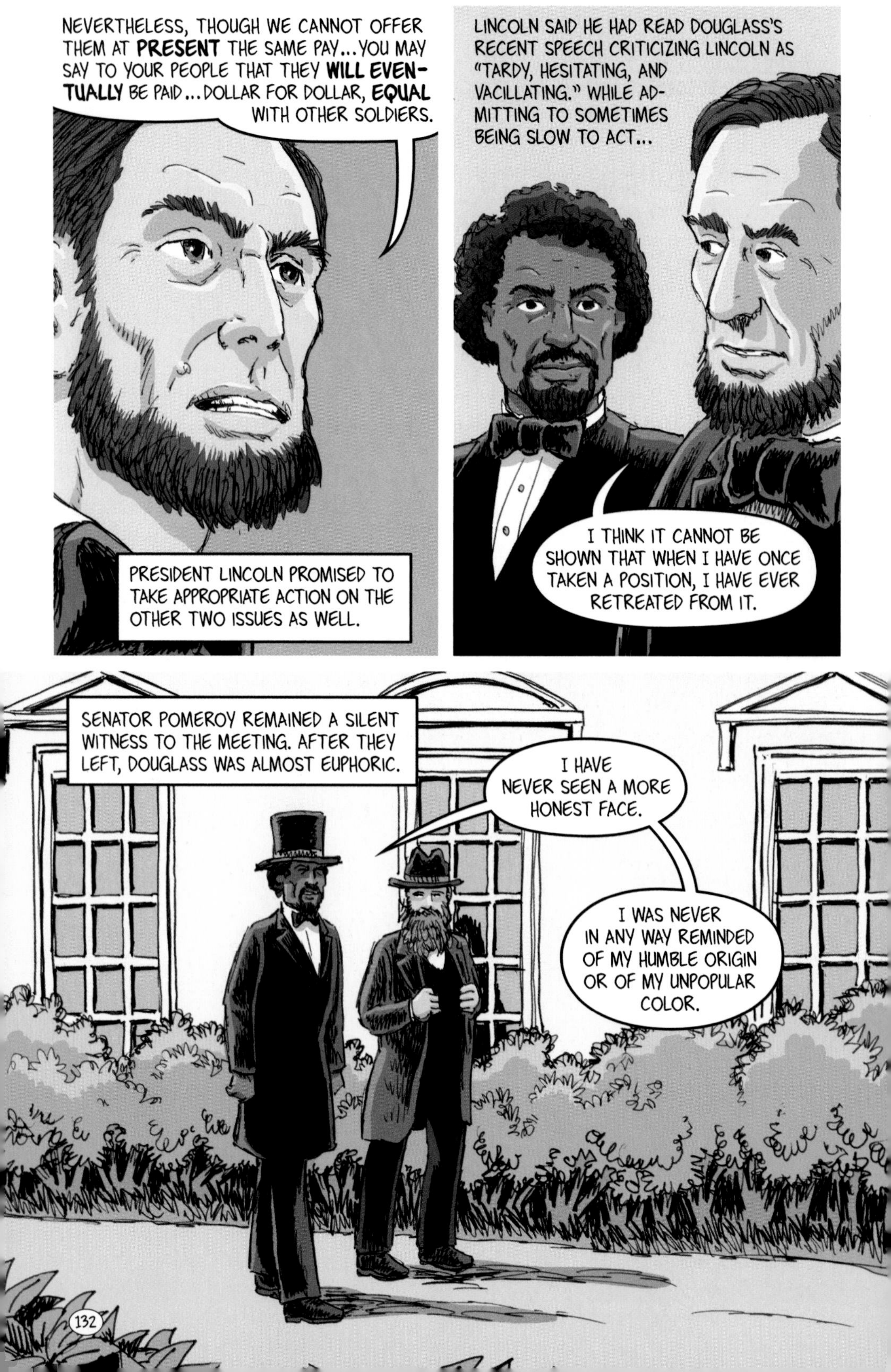
NEVERTHELESS, THOUGH WE CANNOT OFFER THEM AT PRESENT THE SAME PAY...YOU MAY SAY TO YOUR PEOPLE THAT THEY WILL EVENTUALLY BE PAID...DOLLAR FOR DOLLAR, EQUAL WITH OTHER SOLDIERS.
PRESIDENT LINCOLN PROMISED TO TAKE APPROPRIATE ACTION ON THE OTHER TWO ISSUES AS WELL.
LINCOLN SAID HE HAD READ DOUGLASS'S RECENT SPEECH CRITICIZING LINCOLN AS "TARDY, HESITATING, AND VACILLATING." WHILE ADMITTING TO SOMETIMES BEING SLOW TO ACT...
I THINK IT CANNOT BE SHOWN THAT WHEN I HAVE ONCE TAKEN A POSITION, I HAVE EVER RETREATED FROM IT.
SENATOR POMEROY REMAINED A SILENT WITNESS TO THE MEETING. AFTER THEY LEFT, DOUGLASS WAS ALMOST EUPHORIC.
I HAVE NEVER SEEN A MORE HONEST FACE.
I WAS NEVER IN ANY WAY REMINDED OF MY HUMBLE ORIGIN OR OF MY UNPOPULAR COLOR.

LINCOLN HAD ALSO AGREED THAT DOUGLASS SHOULD RECEIVE **AN ARMY COMMISSION** TO HELP HIM RECRUIT NEGROES IN THE WEST.

DOUGLASS RETURNED HOME TO ROCHESTER, **EXCITED** ABOUT HIS NEW **FUTURE**.

ROCHESTE

BUT THE **PROMISED** COMMISSION **NEVER** CAME.

FOR SEVERAL WEEKS, A DISAPPOINTED DOUGLASS **RETREATED** FROM PUBLIC LIFE TO BE WITH HIS FAMILY.

THEN, IN LATE 1863, HE RECEIVED AN **INVITATION** FROM THE WOMEN'S NATIONAL LOYAL LEAGUE, AN ORGANIZATION SEEKING A CONSTITUTIONAL AMENDMENT TO END SLAVERY, TO SPEAK AT **COOPER UNION** ON JANUARY 13, 1864.

I MUST ACCEPT. AND I KNOW WHAT I MUST SAY!

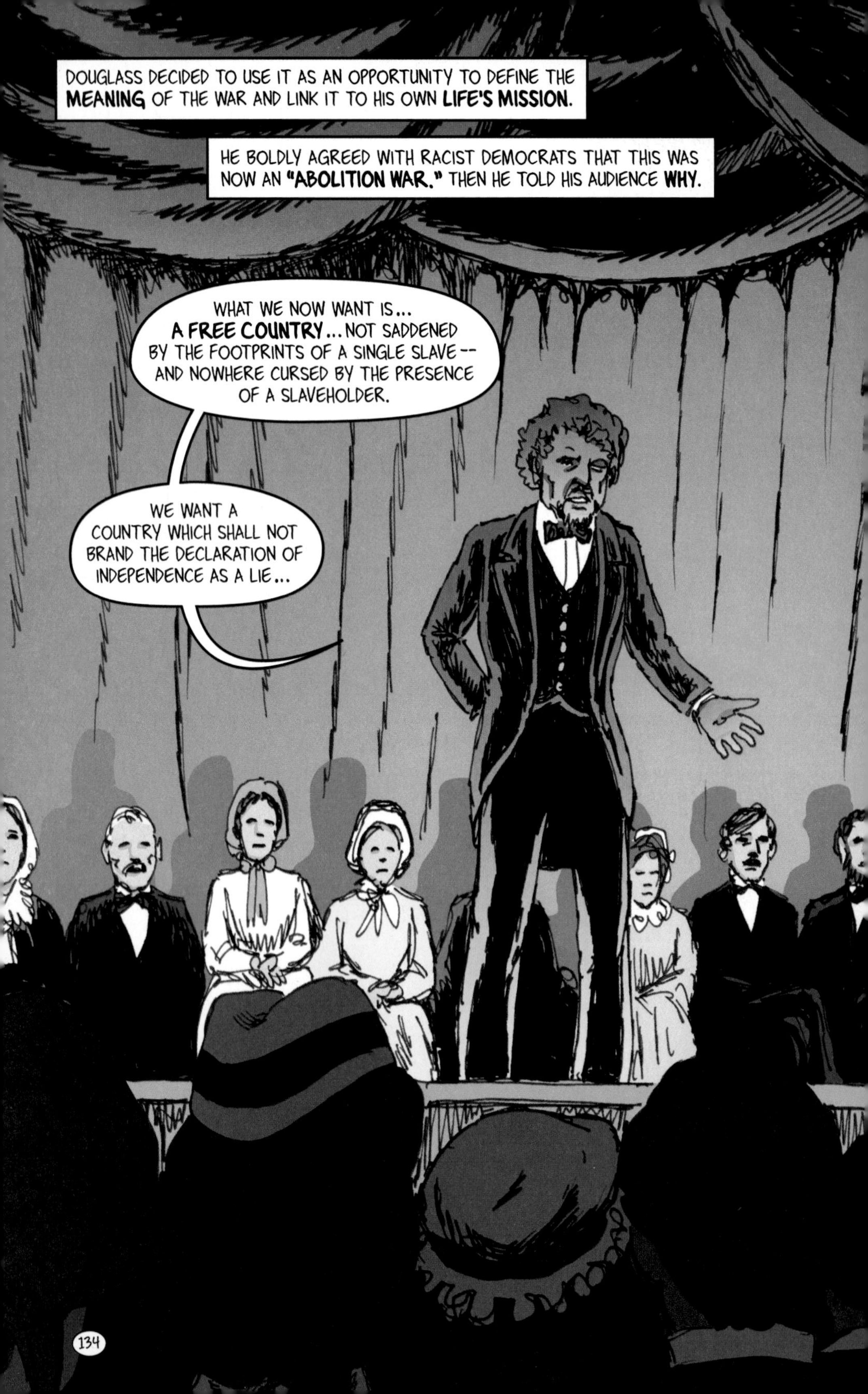
DOUGLASS DECIDED TO USE IT AS AN OPPORTUNITY TO DEFINE THE **MEANING** OF THE WAR AND LINK IT TO HIS OWN **LIFE'S MISSION**.
HE BOLDLY AGREED WITH RACIST DEMOCRATS THAT THIS WAS NOW AN **"ABOLITION WAR."** THEN HE TOLD HIS AUDIENCE **WHY**.
WHAT WE NOW WANT IS... **A FREE COUNTRY**... NOT SADDENED BY THE FOOTPRINTS OF A SINGLE SLAVE -- AND NOWHERE CURSED BY THE PRESENCE OF A SLAVEHOLDER.
WE WANT A COUNTRY WHICH SHALL NOT BRAND THE DECLARATION OF INDEPENDENCE AS A LIE...

WE ARE FIGHTING FOR A COUNTRY...WHERE **NO MAN** MAY BE **IMPRISONED** OR **FLOGGED** OR **SOLD** FOR LEARNING TO READ, OR TEACHING A FELLOW MORTAL HOW TO READ.

SUCH, FELLOW CITIZENS, IS MY IDEA OF THE MISSION OF THE WAR. IF ACCOMPLISHED, OUR GLORY AS A NATION WILL BE COMPLETE, OUR PEACE WILL FLOW LIKE A RIVER, AND OUR FOUNDATION WILL BE THE EVERLASTING ROCKS.

BUT AS THE MONTHS PASSED, THOSE ROCKS SEEMED READY TO **CRUMBLE.** THE UNION GENERALS WILLIAM T. SHERMAN IN THE WEST AND ULYSSES S. GRANT IN THE EAST WERE LOCKED IN **STRUGGLES** THAT -- AT GREAT COST OF LIFE -- ACHIEVED LITTLE.

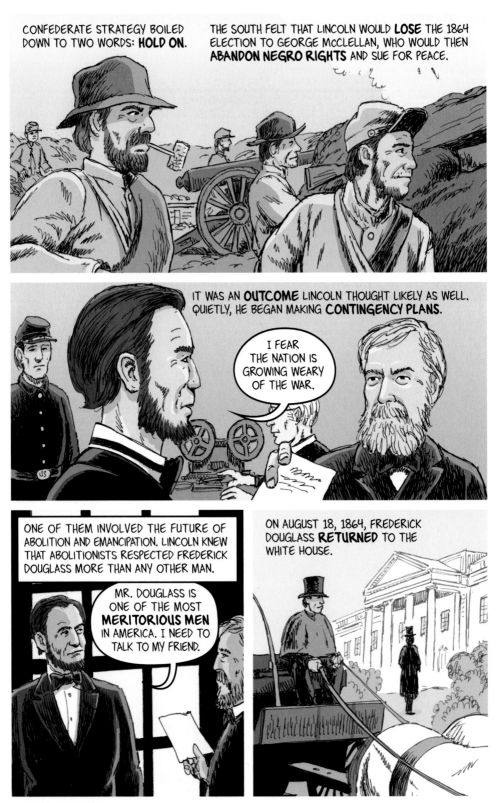

CONFEDERATE STRATEGY BOILED DOWN TO TWO WORDS: **HOLD ON.**

THE SOUTH FELT THAT LINCOLN WOULD **LOSE** THE 1864 ELECTION TO GEORGE McCLELLAN, WHO WOULD THEN **ABANDON NEGRO RIGHTS** AND SUE FOR PEACE.

IT WAS AN **OUTCOME** LINCOLN THOUGHT LIKELY AS WELL. QUIETLY, HE BEGAN MAKING **CONTINGENCY PLANS.**

I FEAR THE NATION IS GROWING WEARY OF THE WAR.

ONE OF THEM INVOLVED THE FUTURE OF ABOLITION AND EMANCIPATION. LINCOLN KNEW THAT ABOLITIONISTS RESPECTED FREDERICK DOUGLASS MORE THAN ANY OTHER MAN.

MR. DOUGLASS IS ONE OF THE MOST **MERITORIOUS MEN** IN AMERICA. I NEED TO TALK TO MY FRIEND.

ON AUGUST 18, 1864, FREDERICK DOUGLASS **RETURNED** TO THE WHITE HOUSE.

LINCOLN HAD WRITTEN A REPLY TO A LETTER FROM CHARLES ROBINSON, THE EDITOR OF A WISCONSIN NEWSPAPER CALLED THE *GREEN BAY ADVOCATE.* ROBINSON SUPPORTED LINCOLN BUT WANTED TO KNOW HOW THE PRESIDENT WOULD REACT TO THE POLITICAL PRESSURES.

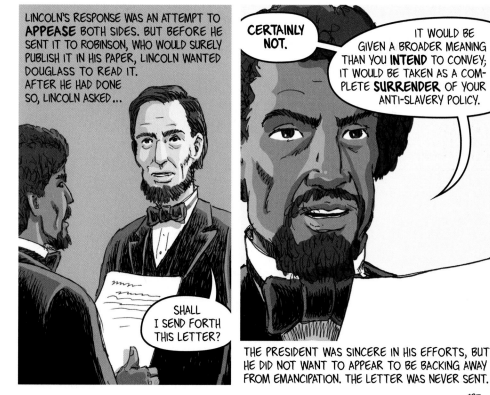

LINCOLN'S RESPONSE WAS AN ATTEMPT TO **APPEASE** BOTH SIDES. BUT BEFORE HE SENT IT TO ROBINSON, WHO WOULD SURELY PUBLISH IT IN HIS PAPER, LINCOLN WANTED DOUGLASS TO READ IT. AFTER HE HAD DONE SO, LINCOLN ASKED...

THE PRESIDENT WAS SINCERE IN HIS EFFORTS, BUT HE DID NOT WANT TO APPEAR TO BE BACKING AWAY FROM EMANCIPATION. THE LETTER WAS NEVER SENT.

KNOWING THAT OTHERS NEEDED TO **SPEAK** TO THE PRESIDENT, DOUGLASS PREPARED TO LEAVE. BUT LINCOLN TOLD HIM TO **STAY**. THERE WAS ANOTHER MATTER HE WANTED TO DISCUSS.

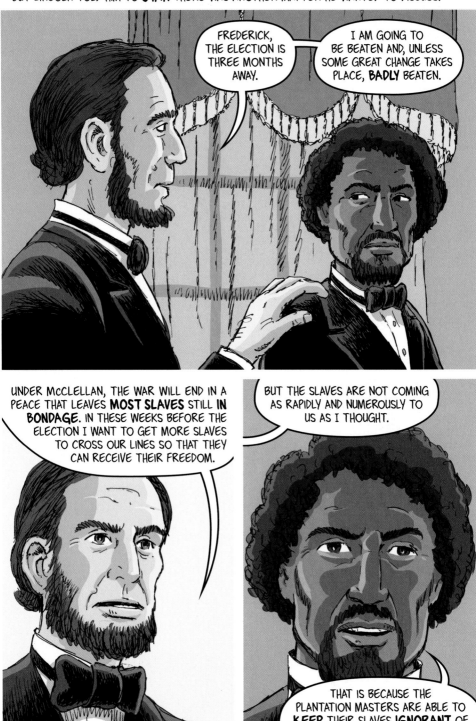

FREDERICK, THE ELECTION IS THREE MONTHS AWAY.

I AM GOING TO BE BEATEN AND, UNLESS SOME GREAT CHANGE TAKES PLACE, **BADLY** BEATEN.

UNDER McCLELLAN, THE WAR WILL END IN A PEACE THAT LEAVES **MOST SLAVES** STILL **IN BONDAGE.** IN THESE WEEKS BEFORE THE ELECTION I WANT TO GET MORE SLAVES TO CROSS OUR LINES SO THAT THEY CAN RECEIVE THEIR FREEDOM.

BUT THE SLAVES ARE NOT COMING AS RAPIDLY AND NUMEROUSLY TO US AS I THOUGHT.

THAT IS BECAUSE THE PLANTATION MASTERS ARE ABLE TO **KEEP** THEIR SLAVES **IGNORANT** OF THE EMANCIPATION PROCLAMATION AND THE CONFISCATION ACTS.

LINCOLN'S WORDS STUNNED DOUGLASS. THE PRESIDENT WAS ASKING HIM TO ESTABLISH A NEW UNDERGROUND RAILROAD IN ANTICIPATION OF LOSING THE ELECTION TO McCLELLAN.

IT REVEALED TO DOUGLASS THE DEPTH OF THE PRESIDENT'S MORAL CONVICTION TO END SLAVERY. HE AGREED TO HELP. THEIR DISCUSSION CONTINUED FOR TWO HOURS.

AFTER HE LEFT, DOUGLASS BEGAN WORKING OUT A DETAILED PLAN TO INFORM SLAVES AND CREATE A NETWORK TO BRING THEM INTO THE UNION, AND TO CANADA IF NECESSARY.

THEN, ON SEPTEMBER 2, LINCOLN RECEIVED A TELEGRAM FROM GENERAL SHERMAN.

WITH SHERMAN'S VICTORY, LINCOLN'S MILITARY AND POLITICAL FORTUNES TURNED AROUND. HE WON REELECTION IN A LANDSLIDE.

ON MARCH 4, 1865, ABRAHAM LINCOLN WAS SWORN IN FOR HIS SECOND TERM. THE CONFEDERACY WAS IN ITS LAST DAYS. HAVING FAILED TO ENTICE THE SOUTH TO STAY IN THE UNION WITH ITS SLAVE SYSTEM INTACT, HE HAD FOUGHT THE NATION'S BLOODIEST WAR AND BROUGHT THE SOUTH TO ITS KNEES.

HE CONCLUDED HIS SECOND INAUGURAL ADDRESS WITH THESE WORDS:

WITH MALICE TOWARD NONE; WITH CHARITY FOR ALL...LET US STRIVE ON TO FINISH THE WORK WE ARE IN; TO BIND UP THE NATION'S WOUNDS...

...TO DO ALL WHICH MAY ACHIEVE AND CHERISH A JUST, AND A LASTING PEACE, AMONG OURSELVES, AND WITH ALL NATIONS.

FREDERICK DOUGLASS HAD WITNESSED THE SPEECH AND, THAT EVENING, ENTERED THE LINE OF WELL-WISHERS TO CONGRATULATE THE PRESIDENT.

BUT WHEN HE REACHED THE DOOR TO THE WHITE HOUSE, TWO POLICEMEN YANKED HIM ASIDE, STATING THAT THEY WERE UNDER ORDERS TO ADMIT NO MAN OF COLOR.

NO SUCH ORDER COULD HAVE EMANATED FROM PRESIDENT LINCOLN...

...IF HE KNEW I WAS AT THE DOOR, HE WOULD DESIRE MY ADMISSION.

DOUGLASS MANAGED TO GET WORD INSIDE TO THE PRESIDENT THAT HE WAS THERE.

MINUTES LATER...

I AM GLAD TO SEE YOU. I SAW YOU IN THE CROWD TODAY, LISTENING TO MY INAUGURAL ADDRESS. HOW DID YOU LIKE IT?

MR. LINCOLN, I MUST NOT DETAIN YOU WITH MY POOR OPINION, WHEN THERE ARE THOUSANDS WAITING TO SHAKE HANDS WITH YOU.

NO, NO. YOU MUST STOP A LITTLE, DOUGLASS.

THERE IS NO MAN IN THE COUNTRY WHOSE OPINION I VALUE MORE THAN YOURS.

I WANT TO KNOW WHAT YOU THINK OF IT.

MR. LINCOLN, THAT WAS A SACRED EFFORT.

I AM GLAD YOU LIKED IT!

TO EVERYONE WHO SAW THIS, THE MESSAGE WAS CRYSTAL CLEAR. BY PUBLICLY TREATING FREDERICK DOUGLASS AS AN EQUAL, PRESIDENT ABRAHAM LINCOLN WAS EXTENDING THE PROMISE OF EQUALITY TO ALL PEOPLE OF COLOR IN THE COUNTRY.

HOWEVER, MOST WHITES IN AMERICA -- NORTH AND SOUTH -- WERE NOT READY TO EMBRACE RACIAL EQUALITY.

LATER THAT MONTH, LINCOLN WENT TO GENERAL GRANT'S HEADQUARTERS AT THE VIRGINIA PORT OF CITY POINT. THERE HE MET WITH GRANT, GENERAL WILLIAM TECUMSEH SHERMAN, AND ADMIRAL DAVID DIXON PORTER. AFTER DISCUSSING MILITARY OPERATIONS, LINCOLN SAID...

I WANT **SUBMISSION** AND **NO MORE BLOODSHED**...

...NO ONE PUNISHED. I WANT THOSE PEOPLE TO RETURN TO THEIR ALLEGIANCE TO THE UNION AND **SUBMIT TO THE LAWS.**

UNION TROOPS ENTERED RICHMOND, VIRGINIA -- THE CAPITAL OF THE CON-FEDERACY. THEY LOWERED THE CONFED-ERATE FLAG AND RAISED THEIR OWN.

LESS THAN A WEEK LATER, GRANT'S TROOPS HAD ROUTED LEE'S ARMY, AND RICHMOND WAS FULLY UNDER UNION CONTROL.

AS SOON AS HE HEARD THE NEWS, LINCOLN TRAVELED TO RICHMOND TO VISIT THE PRIZE THAT HAD ELUDED HIM FOR FOUR YEARS.

BLESS THE LORD, THERE IS THE GREAT MESSIAH!

GLORY, HALLELUJAH!

DON'T KNEEL TO ME. THAT IS NOT RIGHT.

YOU MUST KNEEL TO **GOD ONLY**, AND THANK HIM FOR THE LIBERTY YOU WILL HERE-AFTER ENJOY.

ON APRIL 9, 1865, GENERAL ROBERT E. LEE **SURRENDERED**. THE NEWS SPARKED MASSIVE **CELEBRATIONS**. ON APRIL 11, A CROWD GATHERED AT THE WHITE HOUSE AND CALLED ON THE PRESIDENT TO SPEAK.

SPEECH!

SPEECH!

MINDFUL OF THE GRUESOME COST OF THE VICTORY, LINCOLN TALKED OF THE **HARD WORK** THAT LAY AHEAD. HE TALKED OF THE POSTWAR RECONSTRUCTION -- AND OF GIVING NEGROES THE RIGHT TO VOTE.

I WOULD MYSELF PREFER THAT IT WERE **NOW** GIVEN TO THE VERY INTELLIGENT, AND THOSE WHO SERVE OUR CAUSE AS SOLDIERS.

LISTENING CAREFULLY IN THE CROWD WAS **JOHN WILKES BOOTH**, A FAMOUS ACTOR AND **CONFEDERATE SYMPATHIZER**. THE THOUGHT OF EVEN SOME NEGROES VOTING MADE HIM **MURDEROUS** WITH RAGE.

THAT IS **THE LAST SPEECH** HE WILL EVER MAKE!

THREE DAYS LATER, ON APRIL 14, 1865, BOOTH CARRIED OUT HIS THREAT. HE SHOT ABRAHAM LINCOLN AS THE PRESIDENT SAT WITH HIS WIFE IN FORD'S THEATER, IN WASHINGTON, D.C., WATCHING A PLAY.

K-BAM!

FREDERICK DOUGLASS WAS IN ROCHESTER WHEN HE RECEIVED THE NEWS OF LINCOLN'S ASSASSINATION. CALLED UPON TO DELIVER A SPEECH, HE BEGAN BY SAYING...

THIS IS NOT AN OCCASION FOR SPEECHMAKING, BUT FOR SILENCE...

COMMENTING ON HOW LINCOLN'S DEATH HAD TOUCHED BOTH WHITES AND BLACKS, HE SAID...

WE SHARED IN COMMON A TERRIBLE CALAMITY, AND THIS...MADE US MORE THAN COUNTRYMEN, IT MADE US KIN.

SLAVERY WAS ENDED. SECESSION WAS DEFEATED. YET CIVIL RIGHTS AND EQUALITY FOR NEGROES WERE FAR FROM ASSURED.

THE LAST SHOTS FIRED IN THE CIVIL WAR HAD BARELY DIED AWAY WHEN THE PREWAR SOUTH BEGAN TO REASSERT ITSELF -- WITH HELP FROM **PRESIDENT ANDREW JOHNSON.**

LINCOLN'S VICE PRESIDENT, JOHNSON WAS A FORMER SENATOR FROM TENNESSEE. HE HAD REMAINED WITH THE UNION WHEN HIS STATE SECEDED, BUT JOHNSON WAS A **RACIST.**

PRESIDENT JOHNSON ALLOWED MANY **FORMER CONFEDERATES** TO RETURN TO POLITICAL POWER IN THEIR HOME STATES.

WITH THE RATIFICATION OF THE THIRTEENTH AMENDMENT -- WHICH **ABOLISHED AND PROHIBITED SLAVERY** -- SOUTHERN POWER BROKERS HAD TO ACCEPT THE **END** OF THEIR **"PECULIAR INSTITUTION."** BUT THERE WERE **LOOPHOLES.**

ON NOVEMBER 22, 1865, MISSISSIPPI PASSED THE FIRST **"BLACK CODES"** -- LAWS DESIGNED TO **LIMIT CIVIL RIGHTS** AND LIBERTIES. VIOLATORS WERE JAILED.

FREDERICK DOUGLASS WAS **OUTRAGED.** WHEN CONGRESS RETURNED TO **SESSION,** HE STATED THAT THE QUESTION NOW BEFORE THE NATION WAS...

...WHETHER THE TREMENDOUS WAR SO HEROICALLY FOUGHT AND SO VICTORIOUSLY ENDED SHALL **PASS INTO HISTORY** A MISERABLE **FAILURE, BARREN** OF PERMANENT RESULTS.

CONGRESS PASSED THE **CIVIL RIGHTS ACT** OF 1866, MAKING BLACK CODES **ILLEGAL,** FOLLOWED BY THE **VOTING RIGHTS ACT** OF 1867 AND THEN BY THE **14TH AMENDMENT,** WHICH STATED THAT ANYONE BORN IN THE COUNTRY WAS A CITIZEN.

BUT FULL EQUALITY FOR ALL AMERICANS WOULD TAKE ANOTHER HUNDRED YEARS.

145

FOLLOWING THE WAR, FREDERICK DOUGLASS HELD A NUMBER OF **GOVERNMENT POSTS**, INCLUDING **MARSHAL** OF THE DISTRICT OF COLUMBIA, A POSITION HE HELD FROM 1877 TO 1881.

IN 1889, HE WAS MADE THE U.S. CONSUL GENERAL TO **HAITI**, A POSITION HE HELD FOR THREE YEARS.

ANNA DOUGLASS WAS ALMOST 70 YEARS OLD WHEN SHE DIED IN 1882. EIGHTEEN MONTHS LATER, AT ABOUT THE AGE OF 66, FREDERICK MARRIED HELEN PITTS -- HIS FORMER SECRETARY... AND A WHITE WOMAN.

DOUGLASS SAID OF HIS NEW WIFE, SHE WAS "THE COLOR OF MY FATHER." THOUGH HIS CHILDREN WERE UPSET, IT PROVED TO BE A HAPPY MARRIAGE.

NOW AN ELDER STATESMAN, DOUGLASS COULD STILL DELIVER STIRRING SPEECHES FILLED WITH MORAL OUTRAGE. HE DID SO IN 1883, AFTER THE SUPREME COURT NULLIFIED THE EIGHT-YEAR-OLD CIVIL RIGHTS ACT OF 1875.

THE SUPREME COURT HAS **HAULED DOWN** THIS FLAG OF **LIBERTY** IN OPEN DAY... IT IS A CONCESSION TO RACE PRIDE, SELF-ISHNESS, AND **MEANNESS.**

DOUGLASS WAS CERTAINLY RIGHT. SOUTHERN RACISTS AND BIGOTS FROM ACROSS AMERICA CONSPIRED TO KEEP AFRICAN AMERICANS "IN THEIR PLACE." MORE WORK NEEDED TO BE DONE... BUT IT WOULD HAVE TO BE BY DOUGLASS'S SUCCESSORS.

Epilogue:
"In Order to Form a More Perfect Union…"

FREDERICK AUGUSTUS WASHINGTON BAILEY DOUGLASS DIED ON FEBRUARY 20, 1895, IN WASHINGTON, D.C. THOUSANDS OF PEOPLE VISITED HIS OPEN CASKET AS HE LAY IN STATE.

THE PREDICTION THAT LINCOLN HAD MADE IN 1854 WOULD PROVE TRUE -- FULL EQUALITY FOR ALL AMERICANS WOULD TAKE ABOUT ANOTHER 100 YEARS.

IN 1896, THE SUPREME COURT RULED -- IN *PLESSY V. FERGUSON* -- THAT **SEGREGATION** UNDER THE DOCTRINE OF "SEPARATE BUT EQUAL" WAS **CONSTITUTIONAL**. NEW SEGREGATION STATUTES QUICKLY APPEARED, FURTHER STRIPPING AWAY THE HARD-WON RIGHTS OF AFRICAN AMERICANS.

SOUTHERN STATES PASSED LAWS THAT RESTRICTED LABOR AND TRAVEL. OTHERS TOOK AWAY THE ABILITY TO VOTE BY INSTITUTING **POLL TAXES** AND **LITERACY TESTS**.

IN THE RURAL SOUTH, THE DIFFERENCE IN THE LIVES BETWEEN PREWAR NEGRO SLAVES AND POSTWAR FREE AFRICAN AMERICANS BECAME HARDER TO SEE.

AS THE TWENTIETH CENTURY OPENED, INSTEAD OF THE "NEW BIRTH OF FREEDOM" FORESEEN BY LINCOLN IN HIS GETTYSBURG ADDRESS, IT SEEMED THAT SOUTHERN STATES HAD ESTABLISHED AN "AGE OF NEO-SLAVERY."

BUT PEOPLE OF GOOD FAITH AND GOOD CONSCIENCE WOULD NOT ALLOW AMERICA TO QUIETLY SLINK BACK INTO THE DEPTHS OF MORAL DECAY. NEW LEADERS WOULD EMERGE, A NEW CIVIL RIGHTS MOVEMENT WOULD BE BORN… AND A NONVIOLENT PREACHER FROM ATLANTA AND A SOUTHERN POLITICIAN WOULD LEAD THEM.

ON JULY 2, 1964, **PRESIDENT LYNDON B. JOHNSON**, A DEMOCRAT FROM TEXAS, SIGNED INTO LAW THE **CIVIL RIGHTS ACT OF 1964**. TOGETHER WITH THE VOTING RIGHTS ACT OF 1965, THE FEDERAL GOVERNMENT **FINALLY, FULLY,** AND **OFFICIALLY ENDED** RACIAL INEQUALITY AND DISCRIMINATORY LAWS. WITH DOORS NOW TRULY OPENED, AFRICAN AMERICANS WERE ABLE TO CONTRIBUTE TO AMERICAN SOCIETY AS NEVER BEFORE.

ON NOVEMBER 4, 2008, **BARACK HUSSEIN OBAMA** WAS ELECTED PRESIDENT OF THE UNITED STATES OF AMERICA -- THE COUNTRY'S FIRST AFRICAN AMERICAN PRESIDENT.

THIS WAS **145 YEARS AFTER** THE EMANCIPATION PROCLAMATION. BUT WITHOUT THE COURAGE OF **FREDERICK DOUGLASS** AND **ABRAHAM LINCOLN,** THEIR FRIENDSHIP AND THEIR SHARED GOALS, SUCH A HISTORIC STEP CERTAINLY WOULD HAVE TAKEN LONGER.

I SOLEMNLY SWEAR THAT I WILL FAITHFULLY EXECUTE THE OFFICE OF PRESIDENT OF THE UNITED STATES, AND WILL TO THE BEST OF MY ABILITY, PRESERVE, PROTECT, AND DEFEND THE CONSTITUTION OF THE UNITED STATES.

DOUGLASS AND LINCOLN WERE MEN OF HONOR AND MORAL CONVICTION. BUT IN TERMS OF PERSONALITY THEY COULD NOT HAVE BEEN MORE **DIFFERENT.** DOUGLASS'S IMPULSE WAS TO ACT ON WHAT HIS GUT TOLD HIM WAS RIGHT. LINCOLN'S INSTINCT WAS TO LOOK AT EVERY ANGLE, ABSORB EVERY PERTINENT FACT, SEEK THE COUNSEL OF TRUSTED MEN, THEN MAKE A DECISION HE COULD STAND BEHIND AND NEVER WAVER FROM.

TOGETHER, THEY HELPED CHANGE THE WORLD.

SUGGESTED READING

Donald, David Herbert. **LINCOLN**. New York: Touchstone, 1995.

Douglass, Frederick. **THE LIFE AND TIMES OF FREDERICK DOUGLASS**. With an introduction by Cornel J. Reinhart. Ware, Hertfordshire, UK: Wordsworth American Classics, 1996.

———. **NARRATIVE OF THE LIFE OF FREDERICK DOUGLASS, AN AMERICAN SLAVE**. With an introduction by Robert O'Meally. New York: Barnes and Noble Classics, 2003.

Gates, Henry Louis, Jr., ed. **LINCOLN ON RACE AND SLAVERY**. Princeton, NJ: Princeton University Press, 2009.

Goodwin, Doris Kearns. **TEAM OF RIVALS: THE POLITICAL GENIUS OF ABRAHAM LINCOLN**. New York: Simon and Schuster, 2005.

Kaplan, Fred. **LINCOLN: THE BIOGRAPHY OF A WRITER**. New York: Harper, 2008.

Kendrick, Paul, and Stephen Kendrick. **DOUGLASS AND LINCOLN: HOW A REVOLUTIONARY BLACK LEADER AND A RELUCTANT LIBERATOR STRUGGLED TO END SLAVERY AND SAVE THE UNION**. New York: Walker, 2008.

McFeely, William S. **FREDERICK DOUGLASS**. New York: W. W. Norton, 1991.

Quarles, Benjamin. **LINCOLN AND THE NEGRO**. 1962. Reprint, New York: Da Capo Press, 1991.

Stauffer, John. **GIANTS: THE PARALLEL LIVES OF FREDERICK DOUGLASS AND ABRAHAM LINCOLN**. New York: Twelve, 2008.

Waldstreicher, David. **SLAVERY'S CONSTITUTION: FROM REVOLUTION TO RATIFICATION**. New York: Hill and Wang, 2009.

SUGGESTED WEBSITES

THE LIBRARY OF CONGRESS: AMERICAN MEMORY
memory.loc.gov

THE LINCOLN INSTITUTE
www.abrahamlincoln.org

THE LINCOLN LOG: A DAILY CHRONOLOGY OF THE LIFE OF ABRAHAM LINCOLN
www.thelincolnlog.org

ABRAHAM LINCOLN LEARNING ACTIVITIES AND RESOURCES
www.alincolnlearning.us

UNIVERSITY OF ROCHESTER FREDERICK DOUGLASS PROJECT
www.lib.rochester.edu/index.cfm?page=2884

UNIVERSITY OF ROCHESTER RARE BOOKS AND SPECIAL COLLECTIONS: LINCOLN AND HIS CIRCLE
www.lib.rochester.edu/index.cfm?page=4360

ACKNOWLEDGMENTS

Years ago, when I was an editor at Marvel Comics, a colleague made a comment that I soon came to embrace. Referring to a script on his desk, he said, "There is a quality of doneness here that I appreciate." I can say that that element of "doneness" is appreciated by the writer as well as the editor. Equal to that joy is the opportunity to thank individuals who provided invaluable assistance, support, and guidance along the way. First and foremost among them is our nation's greatest living historian of the Civil War, James M. McPherson, who once again kindly provided an introduction to one of my books. I am also grateful for the assistance of another great Civil War historian, my good friend Craig L. Symonds. Thanks to their sharp eyes and sound advice, ambiguities were clarified and errors were caught and corrected. It was a pleasure to be reunited with my artist for *The Vietnam War: A Graphic History*, Wayne Vansant. Working with Wayne, a longtime friend, is always a delight, because of both the quality of his art and the fact that he is such a kind and enthusiastic soul. Thanks are also due to my editor, Howard Zimmerman, another longtime friend, and my publisher, Thomas LeBien, for their many contributions to making this dual biography a success. I was also thrilled to have Kevin Cannon on board for the digital coloring of Wayne's art. His fine effort has made the project that much more special.

Dwight Jon Zimmerman

ABOUT THE AUTHOR

DWIGHT JON ZIMMERMAN is an award-winning author and producer. His previous collaboration with Wayne Vansant, the critically acclaimed *The Vietnam War: A Graphic History*, received the Gold Medal in the Artistic/Graphic category from the Military Writers Society of America and a Gold Medal in the Photographic/Graphics category from the Branson Stars and Flags Book Awards program. Zimmerman has lectured at the U.S. Military Academy at West Point and the Naval War College. He lives with his wife and daughter in Brooklyn, New York.

ABOUT THE ILLUSTRATOR

WAYNE VANSANT began his professional career illustrating Marvel Comics' *Savage Tales* and *The 'Nam*. Since then he has written and/or illustrated many books on historical and military subjects, including the Civil War, World War II, the Korean War, and Vietnam, and even a story about the ill-fated Bay of Pigs invasion. This is his second collaboration with Dwight Zimmerman for Hill and Wang, the first being *The Vietnam War: A Graphic History*. Wayne is currently working on the second book of a trilogy, *Katusha: Girl Soldier of the Great Patriotic War*, which takes place on the Russian front of World War II. He lives in Mableton, Georgia.